AMERICAN EDUCATION

Its Men

Ideas

and

Institutions

Advisory Editor

Lawrence A. Cremin
Frederick A. P. Barnard Professor of Education
Teachers College, Columbia University

The American Colleges
and
the American Public

Noah Porter

ARNO PRESS & THE NEW YORK TIMES
New York * *1969*

Reprint edition 1969 by Arno Press, Inc.

*

Library of Congress Catalog Card No. 78-89219

*

Manufactured in the United States of America

Editorial Note

AMERICAN EDUCATION: *Its Men, Institutions and Ideas*
presents selected works of thought and scholarship that have
long been out of print or otherwise unavailable. Inevitably, such
works will include particular ideas and doctrines that have been
outmoded or superseded by more recent research. Nevertheless,
all retain their place in the literature, having influenced educational thought and practice in their own time and having provided
the basis for subsequent scholarship.

Lawrence A. Cremin
Teachers College

The American Colleges
and
the American Public

THE

AMERICAN COLLEGES

AND THE

AMERICAN PUBLIC.

BY

NOAH PORTER, D. D.,

Professor in Yale College.

"IT IS NOT NECESSARY THAT THIS SHOULD BE A SCHOOL OF THREE HUNDRED
OR ONE HUNDRED OR FIFTY BOYS, BUT IT IS NECESSARY THAT IT SHOULD BE A
SCHOOL OF CHRISTIAN GENTLEMEN."—*Dr. Thomas Arnold, of Rugby.*

NEW HAVEN, CONN.:

CHARLES C. CHATFIELD & CO.

1870.

The College Courant Print, New Haven, Conn.

ARVINE & SHELDON, Electrotypers, New Haven.

PREFACE.

Many of the thoughts and arguments contained in this volume may be found in four articles published under the same title in the *New Englander* for 1869. Much new matter has been added in relation to the topics which are treated in those articles, and several additional topics have been considered. The interest which the general subject of college and university education has excited in the community, as well as the very great importance of the topics discussed, constitute, it is believed, sufficient reasons for the publication of these papers in their present form. The author has spoken freely of the opinions and arguments from which he dissents, for the reason that the principles which have been usually received upon the subject of higher education have been boldly assailed. The assailants of what has been approved by the practice of many generations, and has been valued in the calm judgment of the majority of candid and considerate scholars, could not reasonably expect that their proposed experiments would be accepted without being discussed, or that extemporized promises or prophecies would be received without being challenged and scrutinized. Whatever has been written in the way of criticism, has, however, been written in no unfriendly spirit. The views which are the most sharply criticised have been expressed by persons whom the author holds in high esteem and with whom he is connected by friendly relations. To prevent any possible misapprehension it ought to be said that while the author has received very cordial sympathy and many valuable suggestions from the officers of the college with which he is connected, he only is responsible for any views or reasonings contained in this volume.

The author by no means regrets but rather rejoices that the attention of the American public has been so earnestly summoned to reconsider these questions, and that the theory and administration of college education have been subjected to severe and persistent criticism. He is confident that the colleges themselves will reap important advantages from this free discussion, and that as the result, whatever is worth retaining in the college system, will be valued more highly, and will be administered with greater zeal and efficiency, and as a consequence the American Colleges and the generous and liberal education which they profess to give will be appreciated more highly than ever by the American Public.

Yale College, May, 1870.

CONTENTS.

I. HISTORICAL AND INTRODUCTORY, ... 9

II. THE STUDIES OF THE AMERICAN COLLEGES, . 39

III. THE PRESCRIBED CURRICULUM, ... 92

IV. TEXT BOOKS AND LECTURES, ... 119

V. THE ENFORCEMENT OF FIDELITY, ... 134

VI. THE EVILS OF THE COLLEGE SYSTEM AND THEIR
REMEDIES, ... 148

VII. THE COMMON LIFE OF THE COLLEGE, . . 165

VIII. THE DORMITORY SYSTEM, ... 184

IX. THE CLASS SYSTEM, ... 191

X. LAWS AND SUPERVISION, ... 198

XI. THE RELIGIOUS CHARACTER OF COLLEGES, . 206

XII. THE GUARDIANSHIP AND CONTROL OF THE COLLEGE, 238

XIII. THE RELATION OF COLLEGES TO ONE ANOTHER, 250

XIV. THE RELATION OF COLLEGES TO SCHOOLS OF SCIENCE, 259

XV. EDUCATIONAL PROGRESS AND REFORM, . . 271

BOOKS AND PAMPHLETS REFERRED TO, . . . 283

THE AMERICAN COLLEGES

AND

THE AMERICAN PUBLIC.

I.

HISTORICAL AND INTRODUCTORY.

The American Colleges have of late been somewhat formally challenged by what is called *the American Public*, to appear before its tribunal, and to give a satisfactory explanation and defense of their system of discipline and study, on penalty of being either condemned or "suffering a default." The challenge has been repeated too often, and from too many quarters, to be wholly neglected, however confident the friends and defenders of the college system may be of the goodness of their cause.

It should be remembered, however, that the present is not the only time when this system has been seriously called in question, or when important changes have been proposed in order to bring it into nearer conformity with the so-called spirit of the times, the alleged wants of educated men themselves, and the demands of what was termed public opinion.

In August, 1826, a detailed report was presented to the Board of Trustees of Amherst College proposing

very important modifications of its course of study.
This provided, among other features, for the addition
to the " present classical and scientific four years'
course," of '" a new course equally thorough and elevated with this, but distinguished from it by a more
modern and national aspect, and by a better adaptation to the taste and future pursuits of a large class
of young men, who aspire to the advantages of a liberal education." It also provided for "a department
devoted to the science and art of teaching ; but more
especially, at first, to the education of schoolmasters,"
and also for " a department of theoretical and practical mechanics." The proposed course, which was to
be equally thorough and elevated with the old, was to
be distinguished by the following features, viz., the
greater prominence given to English literature ; the
substitution of French and Spanish, and eventually of
German and Italian, for Greek and Latin ; the study
of Practical Mechanics ; greater attention to Chemistry, Natural History, to " Modern History, especially
the History of the Puritans," and to "Civil and Political
law, embracing the careful study of American Consti-
tutions." To these might be added " Drawing and Civil
Engineering." Ancient History, Geography, Grammar,
Rhetoric and Oratory, Mathematics, Physics, Intellectual and Moral Philosophy, Anatomy, Political Economy, and Theology, were retained in both courses: In
conformity with this plan, the studies for this parallel
course were assigned to the several terms of the four
years' course, text-books were selected, and it was confidently expected that many who aspired to the degree
of B. A. would prefer the studies which were believed to

be so much better suited to modern ideas. The reasons for substituting the modern languages for the ancient, and for giving a wider range to certain other studies, were urged with great earnestness by the authors of the plan, and they are very nearly like those which we find in the many publications which have been issued within the last few years advocating a reform of the college system. The views expressed in the Report presented to the Trustees of Amherst College in 1826, and those in the Report of. the Committee on Organization presented to the Trustees of the Cornell University in 1866, are strikingly alike. Both reports assert, in strong language, that dissatisfaction prevails extensively with the college system as then and now conducted. Both insist, with assured positiveness, that more valuable results can be attained by providing parallel and special courses of study. The principal differences are, that the Cornell report in its second general course substitutes German for Greek, and in its third, French and German for Latin and Greek, and that it also provides most liberally, and in a very sanguine and hopeful spirit, for optional and special courses, and for a large corps of special and non-resident lecturers. The scheme proposed at Amherst never went any further than to be printed in one or two annual catalogues, with the names of a few special students. No person, so far as we are informed, ever received the Bachelor's degree on the modern course of study.

In 1827, Hon. Noyes Darling, a member of the Corporation of Yale College, introduced a resolution that a committee be appointed " to inquire into the expediency of so altering the regular course of instruction in this college, as to leave out of said course the study of the *dead languages*, substituting other studies therefor, and either requiring a competent knowledge of said languages as a condition of admittance into the college, or providing instruction in the same for such as shall choose to study them after admittance, and that the said committee be requested to report at the next annual meeting of this corporation." In 1828 the committee made their report, and included " in it two elaborate papers written by President Day and Professor Kingsley," one containing a summary view of the plan of education in the college ; the other " an inquiry into the expediency of insisting on the study of the ancient languages."

In the year 1825 a resolution was adopted by the governing boards of Harvard College, in the words : " The University is open to persons who are not candidates for a degree, and desire to study in particular departments only." This scheme was adopted, says President Quincy, " with great expectations, but, as the event proved, without any important success. During these sixteen years, only eighteen students have joined the college under this permission." After the failure of this experiment, the elective system was introduced in 1841, with expectations equally confident. In principle it is not strikingly diverse from that which has been recently adopted. President Quincy wrote a very able and earnest pamphlet in its vindication—not less able in its argument than the very brief statement of reasons in President Eliot's Inaugural, in which he asserts with a slightly emphatic positiveness, " the college therefore proposes to persevere in its efforts to establish, improve, and extend the elective system." The first system was in the most of its features singularly like the one recently provided. In two or three particulars it was less objectionable ; in others, it was more so. It enforced a prescribed curriculum till the end of Freshman year. It then allowed an entire discontinuance of the study of Greek and Latin, with the choice of substitutes in one or more of the following branches : " Natural History ; Civil History ; Chemistry ; Geography and the use of globes ; Popular Astronomy ; Modern Languages ; Modern Oriental Literature, or studies in either Greek or Latin which may not have been discontinued, in addition to the prescribed course in such branch."

The Rules of the Faculty prescribing the details of the plan correspond very nearly to those now enforced, and need not be given at length. The scheme was by no means universally acceptable, either to the friends or the Faculty of the college. It was ably criticised in an article in the *North American Review* for January, 1842, which concludes as follows : " The experience of one or two years will probably show how groundless was the expectation, on which the authors of this system have acted, that a large body of students would be attracted to Cambridge by such a free and conciliatory proposal. Then, if not before, we hope they will be willing to retrace their steps and to stake the reputation of Harvard College, not on the numbers enrolled in its catalogue, but on the extent, accuracy and thoroughness of the education obtained within its walls."

This prophecy was speedily fulfilled. The elective system of 1841 was very soon abandoned, and the college fell back to its old and approved ways of a fixed, uniform, and classical curriculum.

In 1829 the University of Vermont proposed some important changes which at that time were novelties. It endeavored to shake off the restrictions of the class system by exacting an examination upon each author and study, as a condition of being allowed to pass to the next, and it permitted students to pursue single studies or courses of study in any department of knowledge ; restricting, however, the first degree of the college to those students who should thoroughly master its classical and mathematical course. The report of President Marsh insisted with great emphasis, that to give this degree to any others would be a breach of courtesy and good faith, inasmuch as the degree had a fixed and uniform significance. The plan of study proposed was only suited to a college with a very small number of students, and resulted in no appreciable change in the conduct of the university, or in the college systems generally. The high scholarship of President Marsh was in many other ways, however, most happy in the tone which it imparted to the classical and higher education of the country.

In the year 1850 a complete revolution was effected in the constitution of Brown University, in conformity with the principles set forth in a " Report to the Corporation, on changes in the system of Collegiate Education." The measures which it proposed were briefly as follows : " The fixed term of four years or any other term is to be abandoned, and every student is allowed to pursue as many or as few courses of study, as he may choose, subject to certain limitations. Every course of study, when once begun, is to be continued, without interruption, till it is completed. No student is to be admitted to a degree unless he shall sustain his examination in all the studies required for the degree, but no student shall be under any obligation to proceed to a degree. Persons are to be admitted to the studies of the several courses, if prepared to pursue those studies only ; no general examination for admission to the University being prescribed. A variety of degrees and testimonials are also promised." This plan was carried into effect. A fund of 125,000 dollars was raised to enable the University to provide the necessary outfit of apparatus and professors. A considerable addition was made to its teaching force. The introduction of the new system was hailed by its advocates with great enthusiasm, and the most confident predictions were uttered that there was at last one real university in the country which would teach the classics with thoroughness and success to those who might elect to pursue them, and which would also meet the demands and necessities of the very large number who might desire a scientific and practical education. The speedy downfall of the old scholastic system was confidently predicted. But these predictions were not fulfilled. On the contrary, the words which Dr. Wayland had written in 1842, probably with reference to the changes adopted at Amherst and recently introduced into Harvard, were signally realized at his own University. "The colleges, so far as I know, which have obeyed the suggestions of the public, have failed to find themselves sustained by the public. The means which it was supposed would increase the number of students, in fact diminished it, and thus things gradually, after every variety of trial, have generally tended to their original constitution. So much easier

is it to discover faults than to amend them ; to point
out evils than to remove them.   And thus have we been
taught that the public does not always know what it
wants, and that it is not always wise to take it at its
word."   (*Thoughts on the Present Collegiate System*, etc.,
1842.)

We have referred to these facts to remind some of
our readers that the views which are now so confidently
urged are not entirely novel, and that some of them
have already been in a certain sense subjected to the
test of an actual or at least a proposed experiment.
But the lights of experience only shine upon the wake
of the advancing vessel.   The American colleges are,
as we have said, brought again before the tribunal
of public opinion.   This is manifest from the changes
which have been introduced into some of the colleges
themselves, and from the very earnest claim that is
made that such changes are required by the spirit of
the age, the advance of science, and by " the fluctu-
ations of public opinion on educational problems."
Several institutions have already been either newly
founded or reorganized, in accordance with these demands.   We name first of all the timely provision and
the eminent success of special schools of Science and of
Technology.   The Lawrence Scientific School at Cambridge, 1842, and the Sheffield School at New Haven,
1847, began as special schools of Chemistry, and of
Chemistry and Engineering.   They grew out of the demand for special scientific and practical instruction in
the two kindred branches named.   These schools have
steadily grown, and a great number of similar institutions have been provided in connection with the col-

leges, and also as independent organizations. The Rensselaer Polytechnic Institute, established in 1824, had previously done good work in training naturalists and engineers, and had also supplied many of the elements of a general education, but it had not exerted any disturbing influence upon the college system, or attracted general attention. The Massachusetts Institute of Technology in Boston, the Columbia School of Mines in New York, the Chandler Scientific School at Hanover, to say nothing of the many Polytechnic and Agricultural schools which have been founded with the avails of the land scrip of the United States Government, are examples. Many of these schools have added special studies in the Physical and Mathematical sciences, instruction in the Modern languages and in English literature, so as to provide a systematic course of study and discipline in what are called modern studies, to the exclusion of the ancient languages. These courses are somewhat analogous to the college curriculum with the classics left out, except that they usually require but three years and neither require Greek nor (with one exception only) Latin for admission. In this way there have grown up schools of education, upon what are called modern ideas, which it is claimed are more practical in the education which they give, with the advantage of disciplining the intellect to equal power and refinement with that which the colleges impart. The education which is given has been significantly styled by one of its ablest exponents and advocates, "*The New Education.*" The most prosperous of these schools, however, it is to be noticed, have gradually laid aside the irregular system of teaching every student whatever he cared to study, and no more ; and have adopted in its place a regular curriculum, with the liberty of electing between two or more subordinate *courses*, at an advanced stage of progress, and have so far fallen into the approved ways of the colleges. It is claimed for these schools, however, not only that they teach special arts and sciences with more thoroughness and practical adaptation than the colleges, but that their training in the Modern Languages, including the English, is far better fitted for the culture of a large body of students, than the more antiquated and scholastic discipline which the colleges enforce. The doctrine is confidently propounded that for purposes of discipline the modern languages are as good as the ancient, while for every end of æsthetic and practical education, the new education is far superior to the old, in that it prepares the student more directly and consciously for the world in which he is to live,— preëminently because the knowledge and culture which these schools impart are taught with an energy and are received with an enthusiasm which a nearer connection with the actual and impending world alone can impart. The inference has been drawn from these assumed data and from the success of these important schools of science and art, that if the colleges desire to retain their hold on the community, and to retain the number of their students, they must introduce into their courses of instruction many of the newer branches of study, or at least must allow such studies to be elected in place of the severer studies, hitherto enforced as a condition for a degree.

The Cornell University, at Ithaca, has attracted much attention in consequence of the very liberal gifts of the gentleman whose name it bears, the magnificent appropriation to it of the college land scrip of the State of New York, the great prominence with which its concern and the principles of its organization have been urged upon the notice of the public by means of the press, the very great freedom and confidence with which it has criticised the traditional spirit and methods of the older colleges, and the largeness of its promises of improvement and reform. All these circumstances combined with the peculiarities of its organization, or rather of its proposed organization, have been very fruitful themes for a large number of editorial announcements, discourses and advertisements, in which the merits of the Cornell University have been set forth in striking contrast with the defects and disadvantages of the college and university systems which had previously commanded the confidence of a large portion of the Amercan public.

Its peculiar features are, first of all, the comprehension of its instruction under two divisions, *viz:* the division of special sciences and arts in the six departments of Agriculture ; the Mechanic Arts ; Civil Engineering ; Military Engineering and Tactics ; Mining and Practical Geology ; History, Social and Political Science ; and the division of Science, Literature, and the Arts in general. This last embraces *five* general courses of study ; (1) the *Modern Course of four years*, in which "the place and labor usually given to ancient languages" "will be mainly assigned" "to modern languages," attached to which is the *Modern Course abridged* to three years ; (2) the *Combined Course* in which the languages studied will be Latin and German, which is also abridged to three years ; (3) the *"Classical Course"* of four years ; (4) the *Scientific Course* of three years, also abridged to two years ; (5) the *Optional Course.* Different degrees and testimonials are given to those who attend these courses, but the Bachelor's degree is given indiscriminately to all who have completed any of the courses of four years. The qualifications for admission are the possession of a good common English education, and the mental, moral and physical capacity to pursue to advantage the course of study on which the candidate proposes to attend. For candidates imperfectly prepared, special provision is also made, so that " good health, good habits, and a good thorough education in the common English branches, are thus the simple requirements for admission." The scope of the University is expressed in the words of Mr. Cornell : " I would found an institution where any person can find instruction in any study." The features of the University are the following : the practical utility of the education and studies, university liberty of choice, " the absence of fetichism in regard to any single course of study," especial prominence of studies in History, Political and Social Science, the absence of "a petty daily marking system," a close and manly intercourse and sympathy between Faculty and students, careful provision for the study of Human Anatomy, Physiology, and Hygiene, and the absence of sectarian influence, in consistency with the promotion of Christian civilization as the highest aim of the University. The scope and features of the University in general are its signal and certain exemption from the evils which are observed in the colleges ; all of which, it is assumed, can be happily avoided by the sounder principles of organization and of administration by which it is to be regulated.

Harvard College has a second time adopted the elective system on the most liberal scale, and it has begun to advertise freely in the newspapers that its studies "are largely elective." How largely the studies are elective may be learned from its Annual Catalogue ; how wisely, can be determined only by experiment. The students are held to a prescribed curriculum till the end of Freshman year, at which time it is possible for any one to terminate his study of both Greek and Latin, though not of the Mathematics—which is apparently a mere incident of the arrangement of the hours of study. Ample provision is made for the elective study of the three till the end of the course, but it is possible for the student to go on to the end of the course, with his chief attention devoted to the modern languages and the physical sciences, history and philosophy, receiving for proficiency similar honors and the same degree at the end, with those who pursue what has usually been considered the severer curriculum. So far as we can gather from the plan as explained to the public, the election is not between courses of studies having an order and progress defined by obvious characteristics and controlled by some distinct purpose, but it is between one set of studies and another from term to term, according to the capricious or wise judgment of the student. In this particular Harvard falls behind most of the other universities and colleges which have adopted the elective system.

The Michigan University was one of the earliest to deviate from the old and traditionary methods, and its success has been frequently cited as a decisive argument in favor of radical reform. If, however, its courses of study and instruction are carefully scrutinized, it will be found to be on the whole very old-fashioned and conservative in its most distinguishing features. It has a regular curriculum of classical studies, etc., such as is usually prescribed in the other colleges. This only admits to the Bachelor's degee. It has another curriculum called the Scientific in which the French language and special sciences take the place of classical studies. It has another, called Latin and Scientific ; another of Civil Engineering ; another of Mining Engineering. It provides also that students who do not desire to become candidates for a degree, may, if qualified to pursue any study, do so in connection with any of the classes. Besides these curricula and schools, there are the very numerously attended schools of Law and Medicine. The system when closely examined does not differ materially from that of any college which is provided with a scientific and technological school, except that when the studies of the different schools coincide they are conducted by the same instructor. In all of its departments the elective studies are very few, for those who are candidates for any of the degrees in the arts or sciences.

The Michigan University has however been the oft-used text upon which a multitude of homilies have been preached in favor of what is called the university as contrasted with the college system. The number of persons who have been attracted to its professional schools, many doubtless by its almost gratuitous instruction, has given it the appearance of greater prosperity, as a training university in the liberal arts and sciences, than the facts would warrant. Its literary and general courses combined, though very ably administered, have not been preëminent in point of numbers.

We ought not to omit to mention that Union College was the first which successfully introduced and perseveringly maintained the second or parallel course of study, mainly scientific and practical, which has so often been talked of as a desideratum that had been long delayed.

The distrust of our colleges and of their system of education which is now so freely expressed, and has led to many of the changes referred to, has been greatly stimulated, and is likely to be still more effectively reinforced by the zealous and passionate assaults that have of late been made upon the great schools and universities of England. These critical assaults have appeared in almost every possible form, from the ponderous blue-books, that embody the reports of Parliamentary commissioners, down to the spiteful and capricious attacks of titled and untitled demagogues; from the elaborate volume of *Essays*, written by experienced teachers and accomplished Fellows of the colleges at Oxford and Cambridge, down to the ill-natured and ignorant thrusts of half-educated and conceited sciolists and scientists. It is scarce matter of wonder, in one point of view, that some ill-informed persons should imagine that the studies and discipline of the American colleges are the same with those of the English schools and universities, and should draw effective arguments from the imagined uprising of the English people against scholastic traditions, to the propriety and necessity of our doing the same with what are supposed to be similar burdens. It is, however, a matter of wonder that *some* who use such arguments should fail either to see or to confess that the points of difference are so great between the two as to forbid rather than warrant the inferences which are derived from them, or that any one should adopt the motto which Mr. Atkinson has prefixed to his very clever essay—more ingenious than ingenuous as it seems to us—*mutato nomine de te fabula narratur.*

It seems to us that it is only fair for the American assailants of the American colleges to remember that it is only a very small number of the most violent of the English reformers who contend for, or would even suffer any serious diminution from the prominence given to the classics in a course of public education. The Hon. Robert Lowe did, indeed, not think it unworthy of his character to use his fine classical learning and reputation in contemptuously depreciating the study of the ancient languages and the ancient writers, in comparison with the study of the modern tongues and literature. But his was a capricious escapade of a rather uncertain leader, and it should weigh but little when set off against the deliberate utterances of that steady-going wheel-horse among the reformers, John Stuart Mill, himself not a university man, in his inaugural address at the university of St. Andrews. In that address Mr. Mill says: " The only languages, then, and the only literature, to which I would allow a place in the ordinary curriculum, are those of the Greeks and Romans ; and to these I would preserve the position in it which they at present occupy. That position is justified by the great value in education, of knowing well some other

cultivated language and literature than one's own, and
by the peculiar value of those particular languages and
literature." (p. 22.) That Mr. Mill is an earnest advocate
for reform in all the other particulars which his associates insist upon, is evident from another passage which
sums up many pages of illustration and argument. " I
will say confidently that if the two classical languages
were properly taught, there would be no need whatever
for ejecting them from the school course, in order to
have sufficient time for everything else that need be included therein." (p. 16.)

Mr. Farrar also, the editor of the very significant and
able volume, entitled *Essays on a Liberal Education*, to
which we have already referred, says in his lecture before the Royal Institution : " I must avow my distinct
conviction that our present system of *exclusively classical
education* as a whole, and carried out as we do carry
it out, is a deplorable failure." *(Lecture,* etc., p. 18.)
" That Greek and Latin—taught in a shorter period,
and in a more comprehensive manner—should remain
as the solid basis of a liberal education, we are all (or
nearly all) agreed ; none can hold such an opinion more
strongly than myself ; but why can it not be frankly
recognized that an education *confined* to Greek and
Latin is a failure, because it is an anachronism ?" (*Ibid*,
p. 24.) These passages must be accepted as decisive by
those among us who are willing to learn from their own
declarations, what are the real sentiments and aims of
most of the reformers of school and university education in England. It ought not to be necessary to
cite them, however, in order to enable many among us
to judge for themselves what are the methods and what

2

the studies of these schools. Any well informed man ought to know that they are materially different from the studies and methods which prevail among ourselves. We do not say that our own methods are perfect, or that we have not inherited and retained some of the errors and defects which are so excessive in the English schools ; but we do insist that the American colleges should not be confounded with the English public schools or universities, in respect to their defects, as they certainly would not claim to possess all the excellencies which these institutions may fairly assert for themselves.

That there may be no question or mistake in respect to this matter, we will briefly touch upon those features in the English institutions which have been subjected to special criticism in the polemic against them which is now so actively prosecuted in the mother country. The first of these is the excessive attention,—in some cases the almost exclusive attention,—which is given to the study of the classics. In connection with this, the methods of learning and of teaching, especially the enforcement of composition, eminently the composition of Latin verses, have been very earnestly assailed, and somewhat feebly defended. The comparatively little attention given to Natural History and Physics, as well as to the Mathematical, Historical, Moral, and Political Sciences, in the great schools generally, and in the University of Oxford in particular, as well as the preponderance of Physics and the Mathematics at Cambridge, have also been abundantly discussed. The meager requirements for the " pass " examinations in both universities, and the frightful excess to which the coaching and cramming processes are carried in preparing candidates for these examinations, with the decay of the normal efficiency of the tutorial office, and the consequent idleness of seventy per cent.—as it is said—of the residents and graduates of the universities, have been thoroughly discussed and freely exposed. As incidental to these, the excessive development of a taste for gymnastic sports on the one hand, and the systematic indulgence in foolish extravagance or vicious dissipation on the other, have been the subjects of severe comments.

The general neglect of the speculative sciences and of the investigation of principles in their application to all branches of knowledge is also noticed by some very sagacious critics as a defect in the studies of those who read for honors. It is urged with great force that admirable as is the diligence of those who read earnestly, and excellent in some respects as are the results of their reading, yet the absence of a truly philosophical or rhythmical culture is seen in the excessively *sophistical*—in the sense of the ancient Greeks—character of the culture that is attained, as well as in the very extensive prevalence of one sided tendencies in the two extremes of ultra anglicanism on the one hand, and of positivism on the other. The compulsory residence of all the undergraduates, the pedantic strictness in the forms and the notorious laxness of the administration of the college system, with the almost entire disuse of the professorial function, and of university freedom, are topics of almost universal complaint. The remedies earnestly recommended, are the abandonment of the college system, wholly or in part, the allowance of free attendance upon the university lectures to lodgers in the town, and of the freest competition for the valuable honors and emoluments which the universities have in their gift. All the reformers advocate the increase of the number of university chairs, and a very considerable enlargement of the course of instruction in respect to the subjects treated and the range of investigation. A few insist on the abolition of all religious and ecclesiastical tests, and on a reorganization of the whole system of prizes, honors, and emoluments.

It is obvious that while the discussion of school and university reforms in England must involve a great variety of principles and topics which are of direct application to the changes proposed or effected in the American colleges, it is nevertheless true that the American colleges have in some most important respects either escaped or outgrown not a few of the most important evils under which the English institutions continue to labor. The American colleges give great, perhaps excessive, attention to the physical and practical sciences. They give instruction by lectures as well as by tutors. Their examinations are frequent and severe. They do not neglect the study of the principles of metaphysical, moral, and political science. Their supervision of the manners and morals of the students, and their care for their religious culture, are thought by many to be over strict and excessive.

We return to our subject, " the American Colleges and the American Public ;" or, to reverse the phrase, as politeness requires, " the American Public and the American Colleges." The phrase as changed reminds us that it is our first duty to pay our respects to the tribunal before which the colleges are summoned to appear. This tribunal it may be proper for us briefly to characterize without either questioning its jurisdiction or being guilty of " contempt of court."

The tribunal, in the present instance, is both assailant and judge ; uniting generally the functions of the two in the persons of the same speakers and writers. The tribunal, consists,.first of all, of a limited class of lecturers and writers known as *educational reformers,* whose stock in trade consists of a scanty outfit of a few facts imperfectly conceived and incorrectly recited, in respect to the modes of education pursued in the middle ages. It is the profession or trade of these men to assail the colleges of this country as medieval, cloistered, scholastic, and monkish. The study of the classics is denounced by the cheap epithets of antiquated, useless, and unpractical. The study of the mathematics,—which these ignorants fail to see is itself the most unpractical of all, and which it is lucky that they do not know was commended by Plato in exalted language as tending to withdraw the mind from sense and utility,—is recommended as practical by way of contrast, because some mysterious connection is supposed to exist between it and the power to build bridges, to construct railways, and to drive mining shafts. The sciences of nature, as they are called, *i. e.,* the sciences of matter, are regarded as the only sciences which are either real or useful. Physiology from the material standpoint is the only philosophy or psychology that is considered worthy the name. Of literature such persons have only indefinite or low conceptions as a subject of interest or critical study. A traveling lecturer is, in their view, the model of a university professor. Superficial and second-hand knowledge, exaggerated declamation, paradoxical antithesis, and sensational extravagance are the desired characteristics of university instruction. There are but few of these downright quacks, it is true, but of better and wiser men there are many more than a few, who borrow some of the principles and methods by which these charlatans are characterized. Some of these are men of whom we had a right to expect better things.

Another portion of the public who are so ready to prejudge the colleges and their system disadvantageously is drawn from that very numerous and most respectable class of self-made men who have risen to eminence without a collegiate education. Many of this class take the first rank in our political, commercial, and social life, and their success is a perpetual testimony to the truth, that neither a college degree nor a college education do of necessity secure eminence, and that both united must be followed by that practical training of actual life and contact with men, to which the school and the college are only the introduction. A very large class of these self-educated men are painfully sensitive of the disadvantages under which they suffer from lack of early scholastic training. Many of them have labored assiduously and with eminent success to correct these disadvantages by careful private studies in the languages, mathematics, and philosophy. As a class they are the most generous supporters of the higher learning, and of literary institutions as admirably adapted to prepare for professional and business life. Their zeal and liberality in support of the higher education of the country puts to shame many of the liberally educated, who are no less wealthy than themselves. This liberal and enlightened testimony of theirs to the value of a culture of which they feel the need, ought to be received as the decisive judgment of practical men. Others of them indulge a jealous contempt of all disciplinary training whatever, and find in their own success a satisfactory argument for the uselessness of any other than the so-called practical or useful studies, as well as a decisive refutation of all that can be urged in the defense of any other.

Self-made or self-educated men in this country are also very largely connected with the newspaper press ; for the reason that the editor's vocation is one of the most inviting in its rewards to those who have literary or political aspirations. It also promises success in the shortest time and itself furnishes an efficient education in the exercise of the mind and the pen in literary essays. It is not surprising that this class of editors should be very ready to accept any misconception of the college system, which is either innocently entertained or ignorantly propagated in the community. Nor is it very surprising that they should be often tempted to make the colleges and the college system prominent topics of criticism. Many of the colleges are old and respectable from the associations and traditions of their history. They are the objects of love and affection to multitudes in the community. They are the pride and joy of the enthusiastic youth who breathe their exhilarant spirit and participate in their exuberant life. It must also be confessed that they are far from being perfect in their constitution or their administration.

Both of these features make them attractive as subjects for extemporaneous criticism and objects of attack. Whether they are regarded by our imaginative Quixotes, (to whom there is rarely wanting an acquiescent Sancho, perhaps an *Artium Baccalaureus*), as venerable castles that have too long been objects of servile reverence, or as *windmills* which largely fill the public eye—and grind proportionately but little corn—the bravery of attacking them is all the same, and it has stimulated many knights of the press to the pleasurable *adventure* of making the assault. The patent and obtrusive follies of foolish and roystering youth are a very deserving and a very easy theme for severe editorial comments. The aim that could not successfully direct a rifle to a vital point can easily discharge a blunderbuss at the door of a barn.

It is not a little amusing to notice how confidently an old college which has had some reputation for science and culture is coolly depreciated in some ambitious journal as little better than a " high school" in its aims and methods, while some new institution that in more than one sense is not yet "out of the woods" is as confidently extolled as alone following the *liberal methods* of the university. If we ask who writes all this wisdom, we may not always be able to answer. But we usually can say with truth, that it was indited by some one who has never ceased to be vexed at the injustice of the fates which denied him a college education, or is moved with envy at the fancied superciliousness of those who have received a college diploma, or is filled with conceit that he has outstripped, in the honors and emoluments of life, so many graduates, or bears some mean grudge towards the Alma Mater whose good name he dishonors.

Another important element in this varying and shifting tribunal before which the colleges are summoned to answer, consists of the many graduates of these colleges who have received little advantage from their college training, or are unconscious of the advantages which they have received in fact. The question very naturally presents itself at this point, how it can happen if the college system is so excellent itself, that so many graduates of colleges are at the present moment so clamorous for college reform? Nay, how is it that they constitute so large and so important an element of the tribunal before which these colleges are summoned to plead their cause? We will endeavor to answer these questions, premising that we ourselves admit and contend that the college system and its administration require and admit some important changes.

In answer to these questions, we would say in the first place, that many college graduates are not aware of the extent of the advantages which they have derived from their public education. All processes that are properly gymnastic and disciplinary perform a service and impart benefits of which the recipient is unconscious at the time of receiving them, and which, unless he has given special attention to education as a study, he cannot fully appreciate by subsequent reflection. The mental growth to which they contribute is so slow and insensible, that the fact that growth is achieved and by the means employed, is very rarely noticed at the time of its occurrence. Let it be conceded that some studies must be chiefly disciplinary, and it by no means follows, because the graduates of colleges are not distinctly aware of the value of the course by which they have been trained, that the course was not the best conceivable for the very persons who are the least sensible of what it has done for them. Again, every system of education supposes docility, coöperation, and effort on the part of the pupil. No scheme of education can be efficient without these. We add also the very obvious but almost forgotten truth, that no system, however skillfully framed or wisely administered, has ever been known actually to secure such zeal and enthusiasm as is required for the best effects. While we concede that one system of studies and discipline is better fitted than another to awaken and sustain the interest of students, we may safely assert that there are many college graduates who reproach the college system for not having done more for them, who would not have the hardihood to affirm that any selection of studies, any course of discipline, or any wisdom of instructors would have exorcised the indolence and self-indulgence, the careless and irresponsible spirit which possessed them in their college days.

There are others, and these are not few, who were bent on self-improvement in their college life, and were not unwilling to labor, whose want of success was chiefly owing to their very inadequate preparation for its studies. Any course of public education must assume or prescribe some previous knowledge and culture, and those who persist in beginning or continuing their college life without such preparation, have only themselves or their friends to blame that the college course benefited them so little.

There are some graduates, however, who were earnest, laborious, and successful in their college studies, who are disposed earnestly to criticise the course which was prescribed, because it did not fit them more directly for the calling or duties of their actual life. Such contend that a more direct adaptation of its studies to the foreseen wants of the student would awaken greater enthusiasm and secure far more vigorous and successful work. It is natural, when a graduate comes to any special employment or duty, that he should regret that his college studies did not train him directly for it. He may desire to travel or study in a foreign country, or his professional or commercial success would be facilitated if he were master of French, German, or Spanish. He is very likely to exclaim, "Would that the time which I wasted in the tiresome Latin or hateful Greek had been spent in learning the living language which I now have occasion to use !" Or let him painfully feel his deficiencies in the command of a good English style or in familiarity with English literature, and he breaks out into a similar impatient reproach that his Alma Mater did not foresee and provide for his future wants in this particular, instead of cramming him with Greek and Latin syntax and etymology. Or it may be that he is a manufacturer or trader, and he would give twice or ten times the cost of his college education if he were a proficient in chemistry, physics, or navigation. Those who make these complaints leave out of view much which they ought to consider, and especially that it is often impossible to foresee what a man's employment in life will be. Conceding that a college course may be both professional and disciplinary, it might be a worse mistake for a man to have studied German and find that he needs to use only Spanish, than to have

studied Latin and find that he needs either German or
Spanish, or to have studied chemistry or physics when
he requires a knowledge of English or French literature. These considerations bring us back to the old
doctrine so offensive to a few college educated men that
the college course is preëminently designed to give
power to acquire and to think, rather than to impart
special knowledge or special discipline. But on this we
will not dwell at present, but only remind those who
utter these critical complaints that they do not always
think of the very great advantage they have gained for
acquiring German, French, Spanish, chemistry, physics,
and even business judgment and skill, above those who
have not been thus disciplined. Most of all, would we
ask them to notice whether if their sense of the importance to themselves of German, French, chemistry, etc.,
had been as keen while they were in college as it is at
present, they would not or could not have mastered these
special studies, in addition to the Latin and Greek which
the college prescribed. Without such a sense of their
importance, their mastery even of these branches might
not have been so complete as they find to be needful,
and the imperfect knowledge obtained might have been
purchased at the cost of a feebler power to acquire,
understand, and apply not only these useful studies, but
all other knowledge and skill. Why should it be so
easy for a man to forget that when in college he was
something of a boy, and to cheat himself with the fond
persuasion that any system of study would have endowed him with the wisdom and forecast of a man?
Why should reflecting men persuade themselves that
a college training can of itself give the wisdom of age

to the thoughtlessness of youth, or wake up that enthusiasm for self-improvement which experience only can
develop? It is most unreasonable, unjust, and ungrateful, to demand of any system of education or institution
of learning that it should place in the bow of the vessel which rushes impetuously before the breeze, those
glowing " stern lights" which, even for the earnest and
wise, shine so sadly and so luridly over the path which
has engulfed so many good resolutions, so many vain
essays, so many ambitious plans, so many schemes of
study, so many promised acquisitions of knowledge
and power; which path for the vicious and indolent is
but a foaming and dreary waste of ruin.

There are still others, Ishmaelites by nature, who
from sheer perverseness of spirit, or rankling jealousy,
have never ceased to cherish some petty spite or permanent hostility toward their own college and the college
system. Now and then a communication appears in
the public prints, which criticises severely the college
system, especially its disciplinary features, by gross car-
icature and exaggeration of its incidental and unavoid-
able evils. It is generally easy to read between the
lines much more than the writer has penned. To the
signature, " A Graduate," it is not usually unjust to ap-
pend, "who himself was foremost in the petty deceits,
the debasing tricks, and the shuffling superficialness,
which he represents as common to the whole academic
body." The woman who accuses her sex as universally frail cannot herself be very high toned in personal virtue.

We repeat the assertion already made that we do not
regard the college system as faultless. On the con-

trary, we believe it to be capable of some very important modifications and improvements. At the same
time, we affirm that the principal features by which it is
characterized are susceptible of a triumphant vindication even before the somewhat miscellaneous tribunal
which we have briefly described. We propose to consider these distinguishing features, and to enquire how
far they are capable of vindication, and in what respects
the colleges may be improved either in their constitution or their administration. We will consider, first of
all, the studies which should be pursued.

II.

THE STUDIES OF THE AMERICAN COLLEGES.

The American Colleges have been from the first and
uniformly schools of classical study and learning. A
knowledge of the elements of the Greek and Latin languages has been required for admission, and the study of
the two has been enforced upon all, as the condition of
receiving the Bachelor's degree. This has been universally true, the few exceptions being too inconsiderable
to deserve attention. The enforced study of these languages upon all the students, and for the most of the
undergraduate course, is a ground of complaint, and its
advocates are required to give anew the reasons for ad-
hering to it. The trustees of the Cornell University,
while they shrink from the charge of abandoning or depreciating the study of the classics, have distinctly
taken the position, that for the purposes of discipline
and culture, the study of the French and German classics is as efficient as the study of the Greek and Latin,
and that an equivalent knowledge of either two should
entitle the student to the same college honors. The
doctrine is also very extensively taught that it is questionable whether the study of language is better fitted
to train and discipline the mind in early life than the
study of physics or history; and, granting that it is,
that it does not follow that the study of Greek or

Latin is uniformly to be preferred to that of German or French. In short, the mind of our tribunal, " the American public," is at present undecided, and disturbed by the question whether the colleges do not commit a grievous wrong in enforcing classical studies upon all their students, and in giving to these studies especial honor.

We contend not only that the colleges have judged rightly in giving to the study of language the prominence which it receives, and that the Greek and Latin deserve the special preëminence which has been assigned them, but that there are peculiar reasons why they should be even more thoroughly and earnestly cultivated than they have been.

Our first position is, that for the years appropriated to school and college training, there is no study which is so well adapted to mental discipline as the study of language. We argue this from the fact that language is the chief instrument of intelligence. It is thought made visible and clear, not merely to the person to whom thoughts are to be conveyed, but to the person who thinks for and by himself. The earliest discriminations and memories to which we are tasked by nature are those which are involved in the mastery of our mother tongue. It is true the observation required for the education of the eye and the ear and in the control and discipline of the body, involves a multitude of "object lessons," and imposes much " object teaching," but it can scarcely be contended that this discipline of the senses requires either the *culture* or the *discipline* of the intellect, in the same sense as does that attention to language which is required in learning to speak and write the language which is first acquired. We assume, because it is not necessary to prove, that the most conspicuously intellectual of the various intellectual acts of infancy and childhood are exercised upon language. The slowness and difficulty with which some children learn to use language is correctly taken as an infallible sign of some defect or late development of intellectual power. Nor should it be overlooked that the most important part of the knowledge which we acquire is gained through words spoken or written, and that the study of nature itself must be prosecuted to a large extent through books. Natural history, with its curious facts and nice discriminations, geography with its descriptions of mountains and rivers, of distant and unseen lands, and romance with its fairy tales, so exciting and so dear to the child, all presuppose and exercise the same knowledge. The world of words is, in its way, as important and as real to the child as the world of things ; and most of the intellectual relations of either things or thoughts can only be discerned by first apprehending and attending to the relations of words. The world of words is not to him, as is often charged, a world of dead and dry abstractions, but it is the realm in which the imagination weaves its subtle creations, and disports itself in the delights of its never wearied romancing.

As school-life begins and advances, the intellect is tasked and disciplined by special classes of studies, the object of which is to train the intellectual power, and to furnish it with facts and truths. The mind is constrained to reflection and analysis. From acquisition, observation and memory, it proceeds to be trained to the independent judgments of science. What shall be the subject matter upon which its essays are employed? Nature directs, and the experience of many generations has confirmed the wisdom of her intimations, that language is the appropriate sphere of these essays. The mind is not sufficiently matured to study nature in a scientific way. Of *natural history* the mind at this period is capable, but not of the *sciences of nature*. The *facts* of natural history, the experiments of physics and chemistry, do not discipline the youth enough ; the *science* of these facts involves a training and progress which the intellect has not yet attained. The mathematics present a most important field, but this field is peculiar and unique. For the sphere and materials of what we call intellectual training we are shut up to the study of language ; not exclusively, indeed, for, as we shall show in its place, facts and imaginations should both instruct and relieve the excessive and one-sided strain which the discipline of language involves ; but if there is to be discipline in the eminent sense, it must be effected by means of the study of language. Whatever substitute be devised, it will fail of imparting that peculiar intellectual facility and power which this study secures.

Assuming that the study of language is the most efficient instrument of discipline, we assert that the study of the classical languages should be universally preferred to any other as a means of discipline in every course of liberal education, and should continue to be made prominent and necessary in the American colleges. When we assert this, we do not assert it as a self-evident or as an unquestioned proposition. It is a fair question to ask, and a reasonable one to be answered, "Why is not French as efficient an instrument of discipline and culture as the Latin, and why may not German be substituted for the Greek, provided each be thoroughly and scientifically studied ?" This question is fair and reasonable to discuss and answer, because there is *prima facie* evidence that the one is as good as the other. But this *prima facie* probability is, in our opinion, far from being the self-evident certainty which it seems to be in the judgment of our accomplished and admirable friend President White, when he says "It is impossible to find a reason why a man should be made Bachelor of Arts for good studies in Cicero and Tacitus, and Thucydides and Sophocles, which does not equally prove that he ought to have the same distinction for good studies in Montesquieu and Corneille, and Goëthe and Schiller, and Dante and Shakspeare." *(Letter to the New York Tribune.)* With all due respect to the President, we think that it is not only easy to find one such reason, but that many very readily suggest themselves. First of all, it is obvious, we think, that the student who makes "good studies" in Cicero and Thucydides will be likely, in the present state of society in this country, also to make "good studies" in Montesquieu, Goëthe, etc., etc. We cannot take so narrow a view of the nature and operation of a literary education as for a moment to consider it as limited to a four years' course. The classical student who is zealous enough to do well, will not, in the present state of knowledge, and with the facilities which he enjoys, be likely to fail to learn one or two of the modern languages also. If he does not do this in college, should he have special occasion to use them for the purposes of study, travel, or business, he will have acquired the power to learn them with comparative ease and rapidity. If he is to acquire several Romanic languages, the thorough study of Latin will even be a positive gain in their acquisition, so far as time is concerned. Mr. John Stuart Mill goes so far as to assert that the mastery of Latin "makes it easier to learn four or five of the continental languages than it is to learn one of them without it." Mr. Mill would make little or no provision for the study of the modern languages in the university, for the reason that it is to be supposed that a man who is bred a scholar will study some things after he leaves college, and especially such of the modern tongues as he has occasion to use.

They are trite sayings that all modern literature goes back to these languages for its germs and beginnings, and cannot be thoroughly understood without a knowledge of these languages and the life which they reveal ; that not only the roots of the languages of modern Europe are to be found in them, but the roots and germs of modern literature are in their literature as well ; that much of what we call learning is written in Latin and Greek ; that Greek is the original language of the New Testament, and records the beginnings of the history of the Christian church, and the great truths on which the church is founded ; that modern science has constructed its most refined and complicated terminology out of materials derived freshly from both languages, and the Greek in particular. But to all these considerations we shall be met with the reply, that the majority of the men who are educated at college will never become scholars at all, and do not require the education which is fundamental to a scholar's knowledge. We answer that, if this is so, the majority of such persons have even the greater need, and will be likely to make a more efficient use, of the power, discipline and scholarship which classical study will give them, than of the more or less of German and French which they may study in its place. The manifold relations by which a knowledge of the ancient languages and of ancient life is connected with the history which they read, the literature which they enjoy, and the institutions under which they live, make even a scanty knowledge of both to be of constant use and application.

The student of Corneille and Goëthe is also mainly conversant with modern ideas and modern civilization. However exquisite the diction or masterly the genius of his writer, the sentiments and passions are all modern. But the student of Virgil and of Homer cannot painfully translate a few books of the Æneid or the Odyssey, without entering into the thoughts, sympathizing with the feelings, and living somewhat of the life, of human beings greatly unlike those whom he has ever known or imagined, whose thoughts and feelings do not repel him by their strangeness, so much as they attract him by their dignity and truth, and open to him a new world of sentiment and emotion. The people, into whose life he very imperfectly learns to enter, though in many respects so unlike the men of present times, are yet closely connected with them by the civilization, the arts, the literature, the institutions, the manners, and the laws which the ancients perfected and transmitted. We do not say that to receive such impressions as an imperfect scholarship may impart, is worth all the painstaking which the study of Greek and

Latin involves, but we do assert that if these impressions can be superadded to the advantages which come from the discipline which the grammatical study of two languages requires, then this is a sufficient reason why Greek and Latin should be preferred to French and German.

We contend, moreover, and it is generally conceded, that in disciplinary influence the study of the classics is far superior to that of the modern tongues, not excepting the German, which is most nearly akin to the Greek. The regularity and fixedness of the structure, the variety of the inflections, the distinctness of the articulations, the refinement of the combinations, the objective utterances to the mental ear, and the graphic painting to the imagination, when coupled with the wealth of thought and feeling, which verb and adjective, which noun and particle enshrine in words and sentences, all combine to give the classic tongues a supremacy over the languages of modern civilization, which all candid and competent judges have confessed. It is not pertinent to claim, that one complicated and artistic language is of itself equally efficient with another for discipline, especially in the beginning of the pupil's studies. It cannot be soberly urged that one dialect, if it be African or Semitic, is as good as another, provided it leads the mind to analyze and reflect. The discipline which is required for the higher education is not a simple gymnastic to the intellect, it is not the training of the curious philologist, or the sharp logician, but it is a liberalizing discipline which prepares for culture and thought, and which gradually lifts the mind from the hard and dry paradigms of the pedagogue, and the enforced syntax of the class-room, to the comparative judgment and the æsthetic culture of the philosopher and critic.

We find, then, the following reasons why what are called "good studies" in French and German should not entitle a person to the Bachelor's degree ; and why these studies, however "good" they may be for certain purposes, cannot be as good for the commanding objects for which language and the languages are studied in a course of education.

They are not so good to teach attention to the structure of language and all which such attention involves, and thus to train the student to the intelligent and facile use of English, or to the criticism of the same. They are not so good to prepare the mind to learn other languages than themselves with rapidity, intelligence, and retention. They are not so good to prepare for the comparative judgment of the languages which one may learn. The exercise of such a judgment, whether it is employed for the remoter ends of the philologist, or the more general aims of the reflective thinker, is one of the most instructive employments of the educated man. No man can be a linguist, in the best and most intellectual sense of the word, who is not a classical scholar, because the ancient languages are the best material upon which to study language. The student, who has mastered the elements of Greek and Latin, has gone much further in the way to the intelligent knowledge of language generally, than one who has gone far beyond the elements of French and German. This is explained by the fact already adverted to, that the structure of the classical tongues is complicated yet clear, ramified

yet regular, artificial yet symmetrical, objective yet
artistic ; and that in all these features these languages
are preëminent above the modern tongues. Some philologists do not confess this, we know.   They persuade
themselves that an Englishman can be trained as successfully to the reflective study of language, by the use
of his own and one or two modern languages, as by the
aid of the classic tongues.   But we think such persons,
being always themselves classicists, mistake the suggestions of their own insight and science for the insight
and science which they imagine their pupils might or do
attain. · In short, they imagine their pupils see with an
eye and reflect with a mind that have been disciplined
and enriched by classical study.

Again, such studies cannot be so good for the discipline of the intellect.   The study of languages so characterized must be a better training for the intellect than
the study of the languages which task the intellect less,
from the greater simplicity of their structure and their
greater similarity to the mother tongue.   We of course
assume that the two kinds of languages are taught
equally well, and are pursued with equal zeal and
spirit.   This, we think, is possible.

Studies in the modern languages are not so good as
studies in the ancient, for the knowledge of man, which
they directly and indirectly impart.   The man of the
ancient world is a different being from the man of
modern life.   Stately, artificial, decided, clear in his
opinions, positive and outspoken in his aims, objective
in his life, positive and sharp in his diction, impetuous in his impulses, grand in his connection with the
state, heroic in his virtues and almost in his vices, he

stands forth in striking contrast with the man of modern times—the idolatrous Pagan against the spiritual Christian, the self-cultured against the self-sacrificing, the idolater of country and the state against the worshiper of the Father and Redeemer of man. He is always intellectual, impressive, and intelligible, because he is the perfection of the natural and earthly in its purest and noblest manifestations. The man of modern life is weakened and divided, it may be, by the strife of the natural with the spiritual, of passion with duty, of love with selfishness. And yet the classic humanity is not so strange that it repels or overawes us. It moves our common sympathies, while it enlarges our conceptions of the forms which humanity may assume. All that is good in it is the more impressive from its very exaggerated and one-sided character. It successfully conveys what it has learned or felt by means of the clear, beautiful, and positive diction which it always employs. It corrects our special defects of thought, of sentiment, and of action, by the clear rationalism, the simple emotion, the manly behavior which it always sets forth. It even preserves us against its own peculiar errors by the very distinctness with which it avows them, and the consistent energy with which it acts them out. The student of modern literature is always conversant with men who think, feel, and act like himself. The student of ancient literature is confronted with a human life, which in some most important particulars was unlike what he has experienced or even conjectured ; and yet it is so positive, energetic, and consistent as to leave a strong and distinct impression upon the imagination.

3

The modern languages are not so good as the ancient
to prepare for the intelligent study of modern history.
Modern history and modern literature have their roots
in ancient institutions and in ancient life. Modern
poetry, philosophy, and art, were, at the first, inspired
by the poetry, philosophy, and art of Greece. Modern
polity and law were derived from Rome. Modern religion came from Judea, through Grecian and Roman
society. To understand the beginning and trace the
progress of the new developments which these prime
elements of modern history have undergone, we must
go back to their originals, and understand the society
and life in which they were first rooted and germinated.
We cannot successfully penetrate into the spirit of ancient life without mastering the languages and appreciating the literature in which the ancients have enshrined and perpetuated this life. Our modern educational reformers make much of the study of history,
and of the philosophy of history. But what can the
teacher of history accomplish with classes who are
practically incapable of appreciating the spirit and life
of antiquity? How can those judge of his assertions
or follow his analyses, to whom the most important
elements with which he deals are substantially unknown, and must remain forever unappreciated?

The last reason which we give why studies in the
modern are not so good as studies in the ancient languages is, that they do not so efficiently further the intellectual and æsthetic culture of the student. The
evidence for this has been furnished in the considerations already adduced. If modern history is rooted in
the ancient, much more obviously are modern thought

and modern culture rooted in ancient thought and ancient culture.   Modern speculation was born of ancient
speculation, and still recognizes its parentage, as it
agrees with or dissents from the doctrines of Plato and
Aristotle.   The modern materialists scarcely do more
than illustrate and enforce from modern physics the ancient metaphysics of the Atomists and Epicureans.   The
modern spiritualists give greater definiteness and authority to the mythical constructions of Plato and the
masterly analyses of Aristotle.   The images of the
Iliad and the Odyssey are as fresh and as quickening
as ever, and their rhythm is as musical and inspiring as
they have been in all the generations since the birth of
modern poetry.   They have not been superseded by the
subjective tendencies of the modern muse.   The Greek
Tragedies are still pregnant with mystery to the most
subjective and questioning of the moderns who brood
over the seeming perplexities of fate and Providence.
Allusions to classical images, scenes, events, and personages, are woven into the tissue of all modern writing.   Classical art, with its outlines as sharply cut as
the faces of a crystal, and yet as graceful as the undu-
lations of the moving waters, has not ceased to be the
model of beauty and grace to modern art, because the
products of the last have been animated by the living
spirit of Christian love, or warmed and elevated by the
spiritual graces of Christian faith and hope.

The student who makes " good studies " in modern
thought and literature, cannot fail, indeed, of a quickening influence and guidance, but the student who has
made good studies in ancient thought, has made himself ready to occupy his life with a far more intelligent

and refined appreciation of modern thought and culture. As in the order of the culture of the race, the severer discipline of ancient institutions first prepared the way for the more genial influences of Christian and modern thought and feeling, so in the training of the individual on the most generous scale, the pedagogical period is most profitably spent in the ancient schools, before the pupil enters upon the second stage of thought and conception in which he is to live and act, which, however, is none the less truly educating, because it has become the wider school of life.

The modern educators, who claim to themselves the merit and name of being especially broad and enlightened, take, in fact, the narrowest and most limited views of education and even of life itself. They forget that as soon as the student steps forth into life, modern thinking, modern literature, and modern culture will take him almost exclusively into their possession, and will assert supreme control over his education. Under the fair pretence of preparing him for the fields of thought and action on which he is to enter, they confine him from the first to the same round in which he is to walk all his life long, forgetting that the most efficient preparation for a sphere of action is not always made by remaining within that sphere, but that to be prepared most efficiently for the intellectual and æsthetical activity in which we are to be employed, we must be conversant with their germinant forces and their controlling principles.

Against these views it will be urged, that though they are plausible in the ideal, they are impracticable in the real—that it is impossible to bring all the members of a

college class to study the classics with sufficient interest and zeal to make them eminently profitable ; that
while a third of the earnest men may study them with
zeal, the remaining two-thirds will study them with re-
luctance.   Or, as President White says, "When I was a
student in one of the largest New England colleges,
there were over a hundred in my class.   Of these,
twenty or thirty loved classical studies, and could have
made them a noble means of culture ; but these were
held back by, perhaps, seventy, who dreamed, or
lounged, or 'ponied,' or 'smouged' through—sadly to
the detriment of their minds and morals.   Consequently
the classical professors—as good as ever blessed any
college—were obliged to give their main labor to stir-
ring up the dullards, to whipping in the laggards—in
short, not to the thirty who loved their particular
studies, but to the seventy who loathed them."   The
Cornell University will not have things so ordered ; it
will "indulge in no tirades against the classics."   "It
will have the best classical professors it can secure—it
will equip their departments thoroughly, it will not
thwart them by forcing into their lecture rooms a mass
of students who, while reciting Greek, are thinking of
German," etc., etc.   That is, President White would
have us to infer that, in his opinion — and we suppose there are many who agree with him—"the dullards" and "the laggards," the men who "ponied" and
"smouged," would have committed none of these faults
had they been allowed to study German instead of
Greek, and that the majority of every college class
would study the languages with alacrity and zeal, if
only they were allowed to study German or French.

We do not believe this opinion to be correct, and, we think it effectually disproved by the indisputable fact that the men who are *dull* and who *lag* in Greek and Latin, are almost invariably "*dullards*" and "*laggards*" in German and French, in these very same college classes and class-rooms. The few exceptions are explained by the greater maturity of mind and of character with which the study of the modern languages is begun, and preëminently by the better elementary instruction with which it is introduced to the mind, to say nothing of the advantage which has been gained by a previous, though imperfect study of the classics.

Moreover, what was true of the class of President White in respect to the classics was true *eminentiori sensu* in respect to the mathematics, and yet we do not observe that in the scheme of the Cornell University it is proposed to dispense with a thorough study of the mathematics in the several courses, which are different ways to the same degree. Nor is the principle to be admitted that those who are dull in the mathematics are to be excused from studying them because they *long* for the classics, or *long* for history, or it may be, *long* for the lecture courses to the exclusion of recitations. We do not deny that the evils complained of by President White in fact exist. But they are not peculiar to any course of study. We do not despair of a partial remedy of these evils, but are confident that the remedy is not to be found in the substitution of the modern for the ancient languages.

It should always be remembered that the question with which we are concerned relates to the best theoretical selection of studies, and cannot always be decided by the practical results in particular cases. ، What is best in theory will be best in practice, only when it is thoroughly and wisely administered, provided the circumstances are equally favorable. Among these circumstances are to be enumerated — adequate preparation by previous study and training, judicious methods of teaching and discipline, sufficient time to bring the prescribed course to its completion, and a thorough faith in, and enthusiasm for, the value of a study in pupils and teachers. In some of these respects there is room for great improvement, and this improvement, as we shall show, is to be desired and hoped for in the American colleges. At present we are concerned with the theory of the selection and distribution of the studies.

It may be contended again, that if the modern cannot altogether take the place of the ancient languages they may share an equal portion of time and of honor with them. It being conceded that a knowledge of two or three modern languages is indispensable to every scholar who is truly educated, it is urged that the college ought to provide instruction in these languages as a part of its curriculum. In accordance with this view the modern languages have been provided for, more or less definitely and completely, in many of the colleges, and instruction in them is given either in the regular or the optional courses. The advantages are obvious. The student passes from a dead to a living language, as from a Pompeiian to a modern dwelling. The first is artistic and ornate, but its associations are with the past ; the second is fresh and fragrant with modern elegancies and comforts. The sense of a certain or possible utility in the language learned awakens a peculiar interest, especially if the student has advanced several stages from school life and school-boy associations, and if the interests and responsibilities of manhood have begun to awaken and sober him. The mingling of the ancient and modern in grammatical analysis and in etymological research and literary criticism, is in every respect happy in its influence.

On the other hand, it is to be feared that the time for classical study will in this way be seriously diminished, that the interest in, and estimate of, classical culture will be so far weakened, that the high academical tone will be injuriously lowered, and the most important ends of academical discipline will be in a measure thwarted. A still more serious evil is incident to the elementary character of most of these studies as at present pursued. The college class-room is not a place in which to drill to French pronunciation or German exercises. So long as the instruction in German and French is elementary, the tone and dignity of the curriculum must necessarily be lowered. The college course retains quite enough of the *dressure* of the pedagogue already, and the subjection of the school-boy, and the enforced drill of the French and German professors cannot tend to relieve it of these features. No relief can be devised except to require both French and German—one if not both—as preparatory studies, or to make them largely optional, both of which expedients are at present open to serious objections. It certainly is a fair subject of inquiry, whether the study of both languages might not better be treated as an extra or private study, under the direction of a competent professor provided by the college, and whether if the college should furnish such a teacher and encourage attendance upon his lessons, it would not contribute to a more efficient training in both ancient and modern languages.

If the classical languages cannot with propriety be replaced by those of Modern Europe, much less can the study of the English language with any success be made a substitute for either or both of them. Very much is said now-a-days, in a loose and general way, about the study of the English language and literature in our colleges. The critical study of English literature cannot be overestimated, so far as the awakening and directing of a taste for the best English authors are concerned. To this should be added an ample and critical study of the history of this literature. There is no single study for which the great body of the students have so decided a taste as for this ; none in which they are capable of being aroused to so generous an enthusiasm. It is in efforts at original composition and debate that the consciousness of individual power is usually first awakened, and it is by the critical study of the great masters of thought and feeling in the English language that the spirit of independent activity and production can be most efficiently directed and confirmed. It is not easy to arrange for efficient and successful instruction in this department. The criticism of English composition, the training to effective debate and oratory, and the awakening to a genial and intellectual taste for imaginative literature are all included within its sphere. There can be no question that a greater attention should be given to all these objects, and that the force of instructors in this department ought to be greatly increased. It were greatly to be desired that to these studies should be united a thorough grammatical and philological knowledge of the language itself, and of its leading dialects through the original Anglo-Saxon and its various forms of development. But this, which alone is worthy to be compared with any study of the classics for discipline, is a branch of the higher philology, and cannot come within the college course, because it presupposes a somewhat critical knowledge of the classical and some of the modern languages. It cannot, therefore, be urged by any person whose opinions are worth regarding, as a possible equivalent or substitute for the study of either. The utmost that can be hoped or desired in this department is the mastery of a thoroughly scientific English grammar, if such an one were to be had in the English language. But to suppose it possible to subject one's mother tongue to the same reflective analysis which the mastery of a language not vernacular involves, is to overlook the most important psychological fact, that a language which is familiar and early acquired cannot be analyzed before the mind has reached its highest maturity, nor unless it has been especially aided by the study of at least one foreign language. This is one of the truths which experience may be supposed to have settled.

The testimony of the late Dr. Arnold upon this topic is of greater value, because he was so earnest in his efforts to introduce the modern languages into the curriculum at Rugby, and because his method of teaching the classics was so eminently practical and liberal. " The study of language seems to me as if it was given for the very purpose of forming the human mind in youth; and the Greek and Latin languages, in themselves so perfect and at the same time freed from the insuperable difficulty which must attend any attempt to teach boys philology through the medium of their own spoken language, seem the very instruments by which this is to be effected."

Prof. Goldwin Smith, formerly of Oxford, England, and now of Cornell University, writes as follows in his tract on *The Reorganization of the University of Oxford:*—" Though the classics are no longer what they were in the sixteenth century, they are still, perhaps, the best Manual of Humanity, and they are capable of being practically enlarged in their scope and liberalized to an almost indefinite extent in the way of commentary and illustration. I must own that my experience of historical education leaves me finally under the impression that ancient history, besides the still unequaled excellence of the writers is the best instrument for cultivating the historical sense. * * * Modern languages which some are proposing to make almost the staple of education, are indispensable accomplishments, but they do not form a high mental training; they are often possessed in perfection by persons of very low intellectual powers. As languages and instruments of linguistic training the best of them are far inferior to the Greek and Latin, the merit of which, indeed, as organs of thought, is so preëminent that it is difficult to believe that their destinies are yet exhausted. Nor need men be brought to a university to learn modern languages; on the contrary, they are best learned abroad."

We approach what in the minds of many is a much graver question, and that is whether the study of the physical sciences cannot furnish as effective, and perhaps a more desirable, mental discipline than the study of language at all, and whether, therefore, they cannot take its place as a branch of college or university study. It is contended by many that it can and ought. Mr. Herbert Spencer—*Education :. Intellectual, Moral and Physical*—urges very earnestly and in great detail, that all the processes which the study of the languages involves are brought into requisition in the study of nature—that discrimination, combination, and judgment are all tasked as variously and as severely in the generalizations and judgments of physics as in those of grammar and hermeneutics. His argument is more ingenious and plausible than convincing. The author of a very interesting and able Article on "Science in Schools," in a recent number of the *London Quarterly Review*—October, 1867—argues very ably and ingeniously in favor of introducing the physical sciences into the school and university curriculum. He contends with Spencer that, if rightly taught and allowed as large a place in the curriculum as the classics, they cannot fail to discipline the mind as effectively as these, for the uses of society and of life. At the same time he has the good sense to see and the boldness to say that unless they can be taught in this thorough method, they might, for all educational purposes, as well not be taught at all. He reasons with masterly and convincing power against the practice of teaching the elements of the sciences by compends or brief courses of lectures as tending only to superficialness and conceit.

Our own opinion may be expressed in the remark that Natural History should be taught to children and youth in the preparatory school, but Natural Science, with the exception of mathematical and mechanical physics, should be deferred till the very latest period of the college course, and cannot be taught even then with any success, except so far as its fundamental principles, and so to speak, its logical and scientific relations, are concerned. The mastery of its details and even a familiarity with the application of its principles to particulars must, of necessity, be referred to the Special Schools of Technology or Applied Science ; that·is, it must be made a part of special as contrasted with general or liberal training. For example, Botany and Mineralogy with the elements of Geology, especially Botany, are branches which can be acquired in early life,—which is the observing period,—provided an exciting interest can be aroused in their objects. We cannot estimate too highly the habits which are induced by these studies, or the tastes which they awaken and refine. The nice eye for analysis, the attentive eye for research, the enterprise and self-reliance required for open-air excursions, the elevating influences that come from a contact with the purity and beauty of nature, and the habits of ready tact and rapid induction which such studies and researches involve, are all invaluable features of the character, and leave priceless treasures for life. No one can appreciate more highly than we the tastes and aptitudes of the enthusiastic naturalist, whether seen in their blossom in the youthful votary, or in their ripeness in the matured philosopher. We would therefore insist that these sciences should be studied thoroughly in the preparatory education, so far as they are mainly sciences of observation and of fact. Besides

the advantages of which we have spoken, they tend to
obviate and correct certain one-sided tendencies of the
mere student of books and of words. They rub off
his pedantry and take down his conceit. They relieve
the tedium and monotony of the grammar and the dic-
tionary. We might connect with Botany the elements
of Vegetable Physiology, so far at least as the processes
of growth and culture are concerned. There is no objection to introduce at this stage the elements of exper-
imental Chemistry and perhaps of animal Physiology, to
awaken curiosity and stimulate wonder and reverence.
But further than this we would not go, because the philosophical or generalizing power is not sufficiently developed to grasp or appreciate the truths or relations
of natural science properly so called. Science of any
kind cannot be scientifically taught unless it can be
scientifically received ; and in order to be scientifically
received the recipient must have been trained to discriminate and to generalize, to construct and to judge.
The devotee and expert in chemistry, geology, and
physiology, is so entranced with the wonders of his favorite pursuit, and so interested in the processes required for successful research and experiment, as well
as in the products which these researches and experiments evolve, that he cannot conceive it possible that
any mind at any stage of culture should fail to be excited by his own enthusiasm and be stimulated to his
favorite labors. He says to himself and to the public:
" Only give me the same opportunities which the
teacher of words has so long asserted to himself, and
the training which I will effect will be as much more
complete than any which the old systems have accom-

plished, as the products are more useful and instructive. Only give me a college in which Chemistry and Physiology, Mechanics and Geography, Mineralogy and Geology shall take the place of the Classics, and I will produce enthusiastic students and splendid philosophers." He tries the experiment, but the difficulty is still encountered to awaken enthusiasm and scientific power in undisciplined or half-disciplined minds—to stretch a narrow intellect wide enough to receive a large truth, or to understand and appreciate the manifold reach of philosophical relations.

We venture to say that in every instance in which a scientific education has been substituted for one that is classical or liberal, there have been as many failures of the highest conceivable success as are charged upon the colleges. The classes have contained their due proportion of *dullards* and *laggards*, and this not for the reason that such long for other forms of intellectual activity, but because they self-indulgently dislike any activity at all, or are naturally slow and dull, or have been forced—more usually have forced themselves—into studies for which they are not prepared by the mastery of their elements. Scientific and Technological schools, we are confident, do not show a better average of diligence or of success, than do the classical and liberal, where everything else is equal. It will even be found that a curriculum consisting exclusively of scientific and useful studies, if equally elementary, equally long, equally thorough, and equally remote from any foreseen applications in life, will awaken less interest and zeal and emulation, than a curriculum of exclusively classical and literary subjects, and this for the two-fold reason

that the study of nature, as natural history, requires
special tastes, which are as limited in their prevalence
as they are intense in their energy—and that the power
to grasp the sciences of nature is as slow and late in its
development, as it is comprehensive and splendid in its
rare perfection.

The introduction of Natural Science and of Modern
History into the curriculum at Oxford has not sensibly
increased the number of studious or "honor men," if
we may trust a writer in Macmillan's Magazine for De-
cember, 1869, who gives statistics in support of his assertions. "Speaking roughly," he says, "not more
than one man in three goes in for 'honors' in any
'school' at the degree examination ; and it is remarkable that, after considerable fluctuation, the proportion
is nearly the same as it was thirty years ago, though in
1853 the new, and as it was thought, attractive subjects
of Natural Science and Modern History were added to
the curriculum." (*Study and Opinion at Oxford.*)

We contend, moreover, that such a training, if it were
more uniformly successful in its results, would not as a
discipline take the place of that which the study of language imparts and involves, for the reason that it
neither requires so subtle a use of the intellect, nor
one that is so manifold and various. The Physical sciences do indeed bring us in contact with *nature*, and invite us to discover or contemplate her laws. But Literary studies confront us with *man* as exhibited either
in the refined relations of thought and feeling that have
been inwrought into the structure of language, or in
the expressions of thought and feeling that are enshrined
by literature. They are properly and preëminently hu-

man and humanizing studies, inasmuch as they continually present man to us in the various workings of his
higher nature. Hence they prepare us for the more
abstruse and formal study of man, for the science of the
soul in all its forms and applications, as psychology,
ethics, politics, law, and sociology. Man and nature
are alike the works of God. The science of each naturally leads us to God, but surely neither the mechanism
of the masses of the universe, nor the chemistry of its
molecules, nor the history of the development of its
forces, are *better* fitted to bring us any nearer to Him
than the constitution and workings of the soul, with its
manifestations in literature, and its developments in human history.

From whatever point of view we regard the study of
the sciences, especially those which have been so greatly
enlarged in the present century—as Chemistry, Mineralogy, Geology, and Physical Geography, Zoölogy, Botany, with Practical Engineering and Practical Astronomy—the only course which is practicable is to teach
their fundamental principles in the college, and their
details and applications in a special school of Science
or of Technology. To attempt any other course is
alike disastrous to the interests of Education and of
Science. The man who would be accomplished in any
of these sciences, must, in a certain sense, become a
devotee, sometimes almost a martyr, to its cause. He
must accumulate vast stores of facts and details, must
reduce them to classified order, must retain them within
his grasp, must pursue inquiries and researches of his
own, and must be alert to receive and record the reports
of those of others. Hence, other things being equal, he

has the greater need of a previous general discipline and culture. If he is to be a philosopher, in distinction from a scientific artisan, he will gain more than almost any other class of professional men from a preliminary and classical course such as the college furnishes, for the reason that his subsequent pursuits tend to withdraw him more entirely from the field of general culture. The Scientific School does well to supply these defects, so far as it may, by combining with its more thorough training in the special sciences, instruction and discipline in the languages and literature, in history and philosophy, but it cannot give the breadth and energy which the larger and more liberal discipline of the college is fitted to impart. But the Scientific School itself presents the best evidence of the truth that a course of a liberal training is preëminently fitted to qualify the student to make the most rapid and successful progress in pure and applied science. The well-trained graduate of a college with strong scientific tastes, will often in a few months overtake and surpass his companion who has had an apprenticeship of years in exclusively scientific activities. His power of analysis and method, his capacity for easy comprehension, for wide generalization, and for rapid achievement, as well as his greater subtlety in interpreting nature, will all be conspicuous. We are well aware that some of the most distinguished philosophers in the special sense of the term, in the new and the old world, have had no advantages of classical or academical training. We remember that Davy and Faraday began their studies in the laboratory ; but these most gifted geniuses would have shone no less brightly in the domain of philosophy, had they been disciplined in other directions earlier in life, as they themselves would have been the foremost to acknowledge. If, then, the college teaches the grand sciences of nature, in their principles and leading truths, in their elements and their logic—allowing some range and opportunity for those who have special tastes to cultivate and discipline—and then provides special schools in which these sciences may be thoroughly mastered in a scientific and technical way, it does all that it ought. To attempt to bring the two curricula into close relations, or to force them into unnatural and incongruous alliances, is to injure both sciences and discipline, as well as to assume higher functions and a more pretentious name than the college can lawfully claim for itself. That there is no magic—except the magic of pretension—in the name of a university, without a preparation for its appropriate instruction on the part of professors and hearers, we shall endeavor to show in its proper place.

The only branches or departments of study which remain for us to consider, are the Mathematics and General Physics. These two are so closely connected that they may be regarded as one. We have already noticed the fact that the advocates of the so-called useful studies always include in them both Mathematics and Physics, and that the real or technological schools invariably comprehend in their curriculum the pure mathematics, and often require the study of the most refined branches of the same. But the pure mathematics, both elementary and advanced, are the *least directly practical* of any sciences. It is only because of their necessity as the foundation of the ap-

plied sciences and arts, that they are so readily admitted into the circle of practical and useful knowledge.
The opponents of classical and humanistic studies are
heard occasionally to insist upon the disciplinary influence of the mathematics, and to contrast them with
the languages in this respect. Whenever they do this
they forsake the ground on which they usually plant
themselves, that no studies are to be pursued solely or
chiefly for their disciplinary value.

We observe, again, that in our country there are very
few persons who insist on the entire disuse of the
classics in favor of the mathematics. The only representatives of a view so extreme are the guardians of the
Academy at West Point. But even they do not hold
the opinion that the curriculum in that institution is a
model for general education, but only that it is the best
adapted as a training for military life. Whether they
are wise in this opinion is a question open to discussion. We have no occasion to discuss this question
here. The other alternative opinion is held only in
limited circles. The University of Oxford and a few
of the great schools of England alone give excessive
and almost exclusive prominence to the classics.

It deserves to be noticed that in the colleges of this
country the Mathematics and Physics have had the preponderance over the classics, and that of late they have
been rather gaining than losing ground. That they
ought to be retained and cultivated will be questioned
by none. That they ought to be exclusively or chiefly
pursued, is believed by few. The precise proportion
which they should claim in a curriculum, we will not
here discuss. We have already adverted to the fact

that were we to estimate the usefulness of a branch of study by the number of persons who pursue it with enthusiasm and eminent success, the mathematics would fall far behind the classics. It was not only true of the college class of which President White was a member, but it is true of all college classes, that those who dislike the mathematics greatly outnumber those who dislike the classics ; yet the advocates for congenial or utilitarian studies, do not usually recommend that the mathematics should be abandoned, because they are abstruse and unpractical. The reasons are obvious : the mathematics are essential that the students may master what is called science, and must be studied whether they are liked or disliked ; or the mathematics must be learned in order that the mind of the pupil may be disciplined to that acuteness and self-control which the higher scientific investigations and processes imperatively require. In either view, the principle is admitted by those who profess to reject it, that knowledge and study may be disciplinary when they are not directly useful.

Throughout our discussion, thus far, we have assumed that certain studies may be of the greatest value for discipline which possess no other obvious and direct utility. This is denied or overlooked by many ; or at least it is urged that if a study is also useful, this does not hinder it from being also disciplinary. It is also urged that the range of studies which are both useful and disciplinary is so large that no study should be selected for its disciplinary utility alone. We have seen that this rule is not adhered to in the case of the mathematics, even by the doughtiest champions of utility.

We are tempted to add a word here in defense of the opinion that certain studies ought to be pursued, chiefly because of their disciplinary value. Its truth will be more manifest from the consideration that the employments and sports of childhood and youth are chiefly disciplinary and gymnastic in their influence and effect. The acquisition of permanent stores of knowledge is not the best result of the restless sportiveness of childhood, and the unceasing excitements of youth ; they are the sagacity, the self-reliance, the quickness and self-control, and every other good habit which is gathered from those bright and busy years. The school-life of the child and youth is not so valuable for the knowledge which it imparts as for the power and skill to which it trains. What the boy brings away in his memory, whatever be the subject studied, is worth something ; but compared with the many years of study, and the multitude of lessons repeated, these acquisitions are but meager. What he gains in the power to learn, to judge, and to apply are acquisitions that cannot be estimated too highly. The man, when mature, can quickly master the lesson, or analyze the argument, or resolve the problem which would have cost him many a weary hour in his childhood, and he imagines that some method should and may be devised by which the forces of childhood should be more economically utilized. The child, he reasons, has time enough to learn a whole encyclopædia of facts, and it is a pity and a shame that he does not. Only put him wisely to school, and give him the right description of facts, and he will bring away untold treasures for his manhood. Perhaps he may, but if he is not also disciplined to the power to master and hold

these facts, of what avail are his lessons and opportunities ? By the same method of reasoning it follows
that if he learns these facts in such a way as *not* to train
his powers to judge, discriminate, and reason, his childhood and youth, however richly freighted with facts and
information, will have been almost wasted.

We contend that if most of the employments and
sports of childhood and youth are chiefly valuable so
far as they are disciplinary to power and goodness, the
presumption is, that in the studies of school and college life, the same principle will hold good. Unless it
can be decisively proved that the so-called useful studies
are as efficient in their disciplinary capacity and effect,
it forms no objection to a study that its acquisitions
cannot be used. Its acquisitions of the noble sort cannot
but be used. They may not be recorded in the memory
indeed, but they are inwrought and ingrained into the
very structure of the intellectual and active powers, and
they make themselves manifest, not merely now and
then when a fact is to be recalled and a date corrected,
but on every occasion on which the man is called to
think, speak, or write ; to feel, resolve, or act ; to deliberate, advise, or inspire.

Holding these views, we contend that the college
training is preëminently desirable for those young men
who are destined for an *active* and *business* life, and that
these least of all should seek for what is called a more
practical course of study. The disciplinary studies of
the college quicken the intellect and form it to habits
of method, of analysis, and of comprehension. All of
these habits are brought into constant requisition, when
practical take the place of speculative questions, and

men and their relations occupy the chief attention, instead of books and literature. The liberal studies of the college are if possible most necessary to those who by the necessities of their future calling are to be debarred to a great extent from the amenities of literature, and the delights of reading.

It is urged by many that for such, a briefer course is more appropriate than that of the college, but certainly without reason. It would seem that for a life which is not to be primarily bookish or literary, the period of exclusive dealing with books and science · required in the college is not an hour too long. Experience also confirms this impression by the decisive testimony gathered from a multitude of witnesses, that the young man who leaves college at twenty-one and enters a counting or sales-room, will at twenty-three if diligent and devoted, have outstripped in business capacity the companion who entered the same position at sixteen and has remained in it continuously, while in his general resources of intellect and culture he will be greatly his superior.

It is urged more confidently, that while this training should be liberal, it should in some respects be more practical than that which is permitted by the college. Accordingly the school of science or of technology is recommended as preëminently the place of training for those who are to become men of business or gentlemen of leisure. If their career is to be in any sense professional, as of the engineer, the mining director, the chemist, etc., and the time is limited, the school of science is to be accepted, but for a business life, the more generous course of the college, including, as it now does, the modern as well as the ancient languages, is greatly to be preferred for all the reasons which have been suggested, provided the person will take the time and has either the taste or the capacity for literary culture. If he must cut short his course of study, notwithstanding the especial need in his case that it be as long as possible, then he must be content with what a briefer course will give him. If he has a distaste for books and some aptitude for mechanics or chemistry, then he may resort to the school of science and a less rigorous course in the languages and the mathematics. In the majority of cases, he should aspire to the severer and more liberal training which the classical curriculum furnishes. The world of practical life will take possession of him sufficiently early. It will absorb his energies, and modify his tastes, and occupy his whole being all too soon, and too completely. The future man of business or gentleman, of all other men, in such a country as ours, most needs the college training, and the country in which he is to live requires that he should have it.

Thus far our attention has been occupied with the studies pursued in college. We have endeavored to show that the course or curriculum is, in its general features, wisely arranged, and that the prominence given to the classics and mathematics should never be abandoned. These two studies, we believe, must, and ever will, be regarded as the great pillars on which any education which deserves to be called liberal must always rest. The so-called college or university which does not require or presuppose these studies may assume the name of a college or university, but it is true to the meaning and spirit of neither.

4

But while we defend the curriculum of studies that is enforced in the American Colleges, we do not contend that the administration of it is not attended by certain incidental evils against which both instructors and pupils need to be defended by constant alertness and care. There are also many improvements and reforms which can be introduced as the appliances of these colleges are enlarged ; and as the corps of instruction makes progress in numbers, in cultivation, and in devotion to its work. We hope also for very great advances from the improved cultivation of the community and the quickening influences of a higher civilization.

What the colleges need first of all, is a more uniformly adequate preparation on the part of those admitted to their privileges. Any organized institution of learning must prescribe some conditions of admission, whether one curriculum of studies is enforced upon all, whether it provides for many parallel or optional courses, or whether it admits students for a longer or a shorter period. Just so far as it professes to admit all comers at all stages of preparation, and to teach them any or everything which they need or desire to study, just in that measure is it nearer the chaotic or amorphic condition ; or rather is like one of those reptiles which were supposed to be produced from the slime of the Nile—the foreparts organized, and the remainder, as Richard Baxter says, "*plain mud.*"

It being granted that some preparation is required by nature and necessity, and ought therefore to be enforced by law, in order that any course of study may be pursued by even a few persons together, it is obvious that the further this preparation is advanced, and the more uniformly it is reached, the higher and more complete is the work which the college can do. If the grounding or drill work in the classics which is essential to any progress or pleasure in the study of the higher relations of the ancient languages and literature, is not attained in the preparatory school, it must be performed in the college. If the elements of Arithmetic, Algebra, and Geometry are not thoroughly mastered before entering college they must in some way be taught and learned afterwards, at whatever cost or disadvantage. If a part of the students are well taught, and a large part are imperfectly prepared, the college course must be adjusted to the average condition of the class, and the disgust, *ennui*, and negligence of some, and the discouragement and disheartening of the others, will be certain to follow. The fact is notorious that the preparatory instruction in this country is not uniformly good, nor is it likely soon to become so. It is not easy for one college alone, nor for many combined, to bring it up to any desired or uniform standard. So many applicants for admission do, in fact, in a good measure overcome and outgrow the disabilities which are incident to this imperfect preparation, that it is impracticable to arrest many in their course, especially if through poverty or advanced age they have reason for pressing into the college. The door which is open widely enough to admit such persons, and with no very serious inconvenience to them, must admit others who cannot or will not redeem the promises which they make or the hopes which they excite. A brief or even a protracted examination, conducted under the most favorable circumstances, is not always a fair test of actual knowledge, capacity, or promise. Least of all is it when it is applied to strangers under the special embarrassments which attend their entrance into college. It may even be unfair and unjust in proportion to its minuteness and fullness, if it is conducted in the narrow or inhuman spirit of a school pedant or martinet. But the explanation of how it happens that so many enter college without being prepared for its studies does not in the least relieve or remove the evil. It does, however, remove the responsibility from the college itself for doing so much of that school and drill work which it ought not to be obliged to do at all, and for failing to do some of that liberal and intellectual work which is more appropriate to a higher institution. We cannot separate the higher from the lower institutions of the country; nor, again, the education of either from the education imparted by its general culture and its common life. The evils complained of cannot be wholly, nor can they be immediately remedied, by one college, nor by all the colleges united. Much of this improvement depends on the general culture of the community. So far as the responsibility rests upon the managers of the colleges, they ought to employ and combine all their efforts not so much for an ampler as for a better preparation in the classics and the mathematics.

Nor should the improvement be confined to these studies. The incapacity of many students to turn the college curriculum to better advantage, results from their deficiency in general culture and the discipline and refinement which such a culture involves. The power of a college to impart is limited by the capacity of the student to receive and appropriate its manifold educating influences. The incapacity of the student to receive may arise as truly from his ignorance of English Grammar and Geography, of History and Rhetoric, and even of Natural History, as from his weakness in Arithmetic or the Latin Grammar. Not a few students who are entirely competent to pass the prescribed examination with credit,—of the vulgar rich as well as the vulgar poor,—are so illiterate and uninformed in their general culture, and so unrefined in their tastes, as to be almost incapable of taking that higher polish which the college curriculum and the college life are fitted to impart to a receptive and refined nature. If the colleges are to aim to become more positively refining and liberal in their culture, they will need youths whose general as well as special training has been liberal and refined both at school and at home.

No object seems to us more important or more easily within reach than to elevate and improve the secondary or preparatory schools in these respects, as well as in the thoroughness of their scholarship. The most distinguished and the best endowed of these seminaries have confined their attention and efforts too exclusively to the aim of grounding their pupils in the classics and the mathematics. They have made their curriculum too exclusively a drilling process. Abundant studies in history and geography, especially of the ancient world, ought to be connected with the drill work of the grammar and the blackboard. The analysis of Latin and Greek sentences should be enlivened and made intelligible by the analysis of English sentences and phrases as well. The stiffness and dryness of the ancient classics, especially when painfully and slowly construed, would be greatly alleviated by the concurrent study of a living language. The work of Latin composition might be brought home to the comprehension and made easy and familiar to the associations by the daily practice of French and even of English composition and phrase-making. The neglect of all these appliances and conditions of general culture in too many of the so-called classical schools of this country is inexcusable. So long as this neglect continues, the colleges must suffer under reproaches which should not properly rest upon them. The advocates and laudators of our public school system as being so ample and efficient for general culture, ought to inquire how it happens that the system which they assert performs so important a service for the whole community, does not provide the college Freshmen with a more familiar knowledge of the so-called English branches and the English language. Surely the classical schools and the classical colleges are not wholly at fault, that the attainments of so many who have made the circuit of the public as well as of the special schools, are so pitiably low when they enter college.

But the call and the opportunity for improvement, and it may be for reform, are not all within the preparatory schools. The colleges themselves, we believe, may do much to improve their methods of teaching the studies of their curriculum. It does not follow because the first and direct service of this course is disciplinary, that it ought not also to be intellectual and elevating. On the other hand, we contend that, as in the general education of childhood, the disciplinary and enforced should gradually pass over into the intellectual and the

voluntary ; so in the special education of the college
the drill-work should at each successive stage give
ampler and still ampler place for the reflective and
æsthetic activities of the pupil.

In the mathematics there is less room for such a progress. The pure mathematics can never be anything
but a pure gymnastic to sharp analysis, to severe ab-
straction, and, above all, to persistent and sustained
attention. Their charms must always be severe ; the
lights which they reflect must ever be colorless and dry.
The practical uses to which they may be turned in men-
suration and physics cannot divest them of that rigid ·
severity which pertains to their very essence. The
labor ipse voluptas in this discipline comes from the
consciousness of power and from skill in invention.
Upon the principles of the advocates for useful studies
the mathematics should not be enforced at all. But
even on the theory that many studies are valuable
chiefly as a gymnastic—" the *grindstone* theory," as Mr.
Atkinson calls it—it deserves to be considered whether
the mathematics are not carried too far for their highest
efficiency in a general course ; whether excessive tedi-
ousness and painful drudgery are not sometimes the
effects of driving a class into too minute calculations,
or vexing them with manifold problems. The *too much*
is better than the *too little*, but the danger is that a factitious importance may be attached to these studies
which is derived from the axiomatic assumptions of the
self-styled men of science that the mathematics are for
no reason to be curtailed—that the more the student has
of their abstractions, the more concrete, practical, and
useful is his training. The students, not looking at the

matter from this point of view, may not be animated with a kindred enthusiasm for a period indefinitely long. We advocate most earnestly an enforced and rigorous mathematical discipline, but in a course of general education we would not have it uselessly or injuriously prolonged. Let it terminate when its best disciplinary work is done. The college is not bound to yield to the exactions of the scientists, and prepare all its pupils for the *principia* of Newton or the calculations of La Place.

' We would propose that the quantum of Mathematical study should be regulated as follows. In the pure mathematics let the principles of Algebra be taught with a sufficient number and variety of problems to illustrate the matter and to test the powers. The more intricate formulæ and the more subtle analyses should be reserved for honor classes or sub-classes who might accomplish their extra work in the same number of lessons which are allowed to those whose tastes and powers are less decidedly mathematical. Geometry might be divided into the Synthetic and Analytical, the first being required from all, the second from the select or honor students only. Trigonometry and Conic Sections should be required, because both are essential for Physics and Astronomy, but neither should be pushed for the unmathematically gifted any further than is essential for effective discipline. The Calculus should not be attempted except by the few. By the same rule Mathematical Physics and Astronomy should be arranged for two grades of students. Whether the more extended and minute course should be limited to honor students or be reserved as an extra or perhaps an elective study must depend upon considerations which will vary in different cases.

We urge this modification for the reasons already suggested. While the mathematical discipline is energetic and specific in its character, its efficiency is soon exhausted for those minds to whom it is for any reason positively offensive, whether from defect of capacity or defect of early application. We may explain the fact as we will, the fact remains indisputable, that to many college students who are conscientious and diligent, the mathematics are more or less of a weariness and an offense. They neither quicken nor discipline the mind that is forced to efforts to which it cannot arouse itself or is tasked with problems which it cannot master. To certain attainments such persons may and should be constrained, but these attainments should be within their comprehension and mastery. To drive this class of students hither and thither, backwards and forwards, through a maze of which they cannot steadily follow the clue and along thickets whose thorns they cannot avoid, is contrary to the wisest economy in the administration of disciplinary studies. While we cannot share in the depreciation of the mathematics which too many classicists and humanitarians advocate, we do not deny that their best results would be more effectually accomplished, if the intellects of fewer of the unmathematical by nature were less perseveringly bewildered and obtunded by the prolonged infliction of hopeless tasks and demonstrations, in which for them nothing is so clearly demonstrated as their incapacity to master them.

The drill-work of classical study might also be ex-

changed by degrees for those higher enjoyments to
which the ancient writers invite when their works are
read as literature, or are studied with logical or æsthetic
analysis, or are recited with a distinct regard to rhetorical praxis and improvement. Here the question presents
itself, whether the mere grammatical analysis has not
been pushed to a one-sided extreme so as to be over-
refined, unnecessarily complicated, and unreasonably
prolonged ; whether in the modern form in which it is
taught, it is not both prematurely enforced and unwisely
continued ; and whether the importance which is attached to it has not seriously interfered with some
more important benefits which might be derived from
another method of classical study. When we speak of
the modern form of classical grammar, we refer to
those etymological analyses and constructions which
are better fitted to interest comparative philologists than
tyros in the Latin and Greek derivations and paradigms,
and to those syntactical rules which are more easily followed by the philosophical grammarian or the metaphysical student of language, than they can be by the
less advanced pupil. The modern system is immensely
superior to the ancient in its gymnastic results, and, indeed, to those who can compass it, in its logical and
psychological discipline. But it is an open question
which we desire may be definitely proposed and thoroughly discussed, whether this gymnastic is not sometimes premature and over driven, and whether in some
of its consequences it does not supersede very important
influences of classical study, as well as weaken faith in,
and enthusiasm for, classical study itself.

Prof. Francis Bowen's remarks upon this point seem

eminently worthy of attention. " Formerly we studied
grammar in order to read the classics ; now-a-days the
classics seem to be studied as a means of learning
grammar. Surely a more effectual means could not
have been invented of rendering the pupil insensible to
the beauties of the ancient poets, orators, and historians,
of inspiring disgust alike with Homer and Virgil, Xenophon and Tacitus, than to make their words mere pegs
on which to hang long disquisitions on the latest refinements in philology, and attempts to systematize eu-
phonic changes and other free developments of stems
and roots." " Classical learning seems to me to have
steadily declined in this country of late years, in respect both to the number of its votaries and to its
estimation with the public at large, just in proportion
as its professors and teachers have diminished the time
and effort bestowed on reading the classics, in order to
enforce more minute attention to the mysteries of
Greek accentuation and the metaphysics of the sub-
junctive mood." (*Classical Studies*, pp. 23, 24.)

The protest in Great Britain is equally earnest and
strong against the use of a cumbrous grammar—
whether the old or the new—at the beginning of the
study of Latin and Greek, and the continuance of this
use so as to displace the extensive reading of classical
authors and the acquisition of a copious vocabulary of
Greek and Latin words. In the opinion of many, the
cause of classical learning is brought into serious danger
from the two-fold exposures arising from verse composition and "high grammar." Matthew Arnold insists
that as the result of the present discussions, "for the
mass of boys the Latin and Greek composition will be

limited as we now limit our French, Italian, and German composition, to the exercises of translation auxiliary to acquiring any knowledge soundly ; and the verbal scholarship will be limited to learning the elementary grammar and common forms and laws of the language with a thoroughness which cannot be too exact, and which may easily be more exact than that which we now attain with our much more ambitious grammatical studies." *(Schools and Universities, etc.*, p. 266.)

In the best American colleges the grammatical analysis is far more minute, comprehensive, and philosophical than it was twenty years ago. No one can doubt that as a gymnastic it is far more efficient, and that the student brings away from it a far more perfect discipline, as well as a better grounded knowledge of the history and structure of the languages themselves. This discipline has been of immense service to those who have taught the languages to others, as well as to all who have proceeded to the study of special or general philology. It is questionable, however, whether it has conduced to a better knowledge of the Latin and Greek literature, or to a warmer enthusiasm for the reading of the ancient authors. It is contended by its defenders that the decline of zeal and activity in these directions is owing to many causes, and that among them the modern methods of teaching cannot be enumerated. We will not discuss the question here. We observe, however, that since the introduction of the modern system, the lessons in the classics have been materially shortened, and the use of translations has become frightfully prevalent. The lessons must be short, if the whole of each is to be *analyzed* by the student in the class-room. The construing of a short lesson can be easily mastered by the aid of a translation. But to read several pages with a translation must be very onerous, and the indolent and self-indulgent would soon find that it saves little, if any, labor. The superior scholars are soon at home in the more frequently recurring relations of etymology and syntax, and they readily master the short exercises for translation, whether they do or do not resort to an English version. As a consequence, after they reach a certain point of attainment their energies are occupied in other directions. They either tire of classical study, or fail to be inspired with a high literary interest in it. The scholars of a middling rank use translations without scruple, and expend their chief energies upon the ever recurring analysis. By dint of effort they, in a sort, master it, but it is at the sacrifice of what, at a certain stage of the mind's development, is of greater importance to the general scholar. The dull labor on in the same painful round, with scarcely a gleam of light. Poor fellows! *They* get little comfort from the grammar, but perhaps they might learn to read their " small Latin and less Greek" with some satisfaction, if there were more of both assigned them. The negligent rely on their tact at improvising, being guided by familiarity with the teacher's oft returning questions, and hastily run over the short lesson of the day with the help of an English version. We offer with diffidence our own opinion, but would propose, however, that the following experiment should be fairly tried. Let the time of short lessons and of special analysis terminate with the Freshman year or a little later. To grammatical exercises, as a chief matter, and to the hopelessly dull or wilfully negligent who have failed thoroughly to master them, we would say, " There is a time for all things ; the grammar has had its chance for you, and you have had your chance at the grammar." Let both go their own way. They must give way to something better : χαιρέτωσαν. For the remainder of the course let the lessons be very long in comparatively easy Latin and Greek authors. Let them be so long that the use of translations shall be either superfluous or even burdensome. Let the "*ponies*" and the "*pigmies*" who ride upon them, be fairly drowned out by the quantity of the text which is assigned to be read. Let the attention be directed to the import of the matter, to the logical connections and transitions of the thoughts, to the peculiarities of diction, and to a constant praxis in felicitous and idiomatic English rendering ; the possibility being always held in reserve and not sparingly applied, of exposing presumption and neglect by test questions in respect to grammar or meaning. Let the examinations be rigid upon the instructions and analyses of the teacher, and let rapid and current reading be encouraged, with frequent reviews, for the sake of enlarging one's vocabulary. Let reading by phrases and by the eye, without reconstructing the words after the English order, be recommended and enforced. Let an intellectual spirit, and an æsthetic feeling for the peculiarities in thought and diction of the author read, be earnestly fostered. It seems to us that the experiment deserves to be tried, and that it could not fail to be attended with gratifying success. Should this experiment be thought too radical, it might be tried occasionally, by giving up to it the whole or a part of a college term. Or after the end of the Freshman year the two descriptions of lessons and examinations might be interchanged ; longer or shorter periods being allotted to each, at the instructor's discretion.

The question also deserves to be considered whether the interests of classical education have not suffered very seriously by commencing the study of Latin and Greek too early, and thus burdening the school and college life with a tedium and monotony inseparable from early school lessons in languages remote from familiar associations, and from the continuance of lessons in the same language for a period of ten or twelve years. If classical studies were delayed to the age of fourteen or fifteen, and meanwhile the youths were thoroughly drilled in a single living language, and taught to write and speak it correctly and readily, the Latin and Greek themselves would be commenced with very great advantage, and would be prosecuted with a far more intelligent and freshened interest. We are quite certain, that, so far as the objections to the study of the classics have any show of reason, they are derived from imperfect methods of teaching and studying. Such objections can be effectually answered by a change in these methods ; and he is the truest friend to classical culture and college discipline who holds himself ready to consider how far such changes are expedient or practicable. Our interest in this matter arises from our desire that a new enthusiasm may be kindled in classical studies. We are especially desirous that the taste for Greek literature, and the interest in the Greek language, should be fostered in the colleges of this country, as one of the essential conditions of a generous and refined culture. The Latin language is so much more thoroughly mastered as less to need fostering care.

We trust that the classical teachers will not be

offended that we invite their earnest attention to the
suggestions which we have offered.   It is neither to be
disguised nor denied that for many reasons the confidence of many of our best students in the value of classical studies as pursued in our colleges has, of late, been
seriously impaired.   The protraction of the school
method, the imposition of difficult authors, the confine-
ment of the attention for years to refined grammatical
subtleties, and above all the failure to encourage the
habit of *the current reading of easy authors in large
quantities, with chief attention to the meaning, and constantly to .require a free, facile rendering into idiomatic
English,* are in part, not wholly, the explanation of this
decay of enthusiasm for classical study as a literary
discipline.   The disciplinary and the philological results
of the classical course were never so effective and valuable as at present.   Its literary advantages and what may
be called its indirect influence were never greater.
What we desire to see reinforced is its direct influence
in inspiring a love for the best classical authors
and in imparting an enthusiastic desire to read them
fluently.   We see no reason why, with the greatly increased facilities for a thorough grammatical preparation and with the admirable philological and grammatical instruction of the Freshman year, this most desirable result may not be effected.   By *current reading* we
mean first, the reading by the eye without the necessity
of transposing the words out of their succession ; literally *dislocating* them in more than one sense of the
word, in order to replace them, in the English order—
which in this instance is to displace them ; second, we
mean the habit of reading without translating the words
into the English equivalents.   This implies a complete

familiarity with the common vocabulary of the author read. Facility in these two particulars would of necessity involve the capacity to reproduce the sentences of the author in idiomatic if not elegant English, and the habit of current reading would impart facility in idiomatic and felicitous rendering. Habits of reading in this way would favor, if they did not compel, a direct and constant attention to the meaning of the author—to his opinions and arguments if the treatise is logical, to his imagery and diction, and also his sentiments and feelings, if he is an historian or poet. To the formation of these habits of classical reading and the achievement of these objects, the authors selected must at first be comparatively easy, the lessons must be long, and there must be enforced in the preparation for the class-room a constant and comprehensive attention to every matter in which a literary critic and a liberal student ought to be interested. Most of all, the habit of frequently reviewing a single easy treatise must be insisted on and secured so far as is possible by every form of recommendation that can be reiterated and by every device that can be suggested to make the recommendation effectual. We cite the record of the experience of *Daniel Wyttenbach* when he returned to the study of Greek a second time. " I took out of a corner Plutarch's treatise on the Education of Boys, and read it once and again, with much effort, but little pleasure. Then I went over with Herodian, which afforded me a little more enjoyment, but was far from satisfying my mind. I accidentally found, elsewhere, Xenophon's Memorabilia, Ernesti's edition, which I had before known only by name. I was captivated with the indescribable sweetness of that author. The grounds of it I better understood afterwards. In studying this treatise, I made it a point never to begin a section without re-perusing the preceding ; nor a chapter or book, without studying the preceding chapter and book a second time. Having, at length, completed the work in this manner, I again read the whole in course. It occupied me almost three months ; but such unceasing repetition was most serviceable to me."

How serviceable it proved can best be told in his own words : " All the works of Xenophon, the Memorabilia excepted, I read four times in four months. I now thought that I could read any author with equal ease. I took up Demosthenes. I had a copy without a Latin translation, but accompanied by the Greek notes of Jerome Wolf. Darkness itself! But I had learned not to be frightened in setting out. I went on. I found greater difficulties than I had ever had before, both in the words, and in the length of the sentences. At last, with much ado, I reached the end of the first Olynthiac. I then read it a second and a third time. Every thing now appeared plain and clear. Still, I did not yet perceive the fire of eloquence for which he is distinguished. I hesitated whether to proceed to the second oration, or again read the first. I resolved to do the latter. How salutary are the effects of such a review! As I read, an altogether new and unknown feeling took possession of me. In perusing other authors, my pleasure had arisen from a perception of the thoughts and words, or from a consciousness of my own progress. Now, an extraordinary feeling pervaded my mind, and increased with every fresh perusal. I saw the orator on fire, in anguish, impetuously borne forward. I was inflamed also, and carried on upon the same tide. I was conscious of a new elevation of soul, and was no longer the same individual. I seemed myself to be Demosthenes, standing on the bema, pouring forth this oration, and urging the Athenians to emulate the bravery and glory of their ancestors. Neither did I read silently, as I had begun, but with a loud voice, to which I was secretly impelled by the force and fervor of the sentiments, as well as by the power of oratorical rhythm. In this manner I read, in the course of three months, most of the orations of Demosthenes. My ability to understand an author being thus increased, I took more delight in Homer, whom I soon finished. Afterwards I studied other great authors, with far more profit."

These words seem to us to be golden words, and to contain the suggestion of a plan of classical instruction and study which may be enforced with the greatest advantage in the more advanced classes of the American Colleges. While no friend of a sound education would be willing to strike or lower the flag of classical study and culture, at the demand of illiterate utilitarians, it deserves to be asked whether we shall not raise it still higher and fling it more defiantly to the breeze. Let the classics be so studied in our higher classes that they shall be loved and admired as literature, and they will need no argument for their vindication.

But we have lingered too long upon this topic. We proceed to consider some of the more general peculiarities of the American Colleges.

III.

THE PRESCRIBED CURRICULUM.

The first peculiarity which we shall notice, is that the same course of study has been uniformly *prescribed* as a condition for the Bachelor's degree. We say " *uniformly,*" for the exceptions have been so few as scarcely to deserve to be named, and any deviations, when allowed for a time, have very soon been abandoned. When we say " *has been,*" we do not include the few years which have just elapsed, within which some influential colleges have abandoned, in part, a prescribed and uniform curriculum, and introduced very largely, the system of elective or optional courses of study. The period in which we are now living is eminently one of reconstruction and experiment, and with its tendencies and movements the colleges seem to have largely sympathized. The college which we describe is not the college of the passing year, or of the current five years, but the college of past years, and of the present generation.

The theory of education, after which a curriculum of study has been prescribed, has been, that certain studies (among which the classics and mathematics are prominent) are best fitted to prepare a man for the most efficient and successful discharge of public duty. By " public dnty" we do not mean merely professional duty, but duty in that relatively commanding position, which a thoroughly cultured man is fitted to occupy. By a thoroughly cultured man we mean a man who has been trained to know himself in his constitution, his duties, and his powers; to know society in its history and institutions, its literature and art; and to know nature in its developments and scientific relations. The liberal education which the colleges have uniformly proposed to give is none other than what Milton calls the " complete and generous education," that " fits a man to perform justly, skillfully, and magnanimously, all the offices, both private and public, of peace and war." It is a very serious mistake to say that, historically considered, the education for which the colleges arranged their preparatory curriculum was what is technically called a professional education, and that these studies are especially necessary for persons destined to one of the three learned professions. It is doubtless true, that the studies of the English universities, from which the American colleges are historically derived, were originally arranged with special reference to the clerical profession, and that to this day some of the peculiarities thus induced have not been entirely outgrown. The first American colleges were also primarily founded as training schools for the clergy, but as the other professions came to require a liberal culture, this special reference to the clerical profession was laid aside. It would be more exact to say that these universities and colleges were at first designed to give a professional as well as a liberal education. To use the language current in the United States, they combined the function of the professional school with that now assigned to the college. But the English universities and the American colleges were also designed, from an early period, to educate gentlemen as well as scholars. But inasmuch as in the earlier, and in that respect at least the better days, every gentleman was supposed to take some position in society as a legislator or magistrate, a diplomat or soldier, the same education was deemed suitable for all who aspired to what we have called a public position. These liberal studies were not thought unsuitable even for the duties and station of a merchant, especially of one who might be a prince among his fellow merchants in generous tastes, wide information, courtly manners, and refined accomplishments. Moreover, it ought never to be forgotten that the natural sciences were never formally excluded from the scheme of university studies. Even the scholastics included in their scheme of liberal knowledge the sciences of nature then received, and made an acquaintance with them an essential element of the liberal education of their times. The American colleges have done the same from the earliest period. They have never, either in form or in fact, excluded these sciences. Nor is the question now mooted in any of them whether these sciences shall be excluded from the liberal share which they possess of the curriculum. It is whether these sciences are to give law to all the others, whether they shall either occupy the entire field of liberal culture or direct the selection of studies in their own exclusive interest, so that the classics shall give way to French and German, because these last are more essential to the student of nature, and are, as is contended, equally well adapted to general culture.

We contend that the American colleges have been in
the right in requiring a prescribed course of study as
the condition for a degree.   In support of this opinion
we shall offer no extended argument in addition to those
we have already presented, but shall occupy ourselves
chiefly with the arguments that are urged against it.
If the considerations already urged are admitted to be
pertinent and convincing, our argument is complete.
If it be conceded that the studies which have been
usually prescribed in the American colleges are the
best fitted to impart a liberal culture, then it follows
that the practice of these colleges in making them the
ordinary conditions for the first degree is well grounded
and ought to be adhered to.   If our argument concerning the theory of the curriculum of studies is valid,
then these studies ought to be prescribed.   There is
not a single study that is superfluous.   Not one should
be displaced, because not one can be spared.   The
theory of this curriculum has been to provide for all
those studies which could properly find a place in a
system of liberal culture, or should enter into the
scheme of a complete and generous education.   The
end has not been to train men for the learned professions as such, but to train for that position in life
which many others besides professional men should
aim to occupy.   For such a position the curriculum has
been arranged, not by theorists in education, nor by the
traditional adherents to an hereditary system made sacred by hallowed associations, but under the just demands of public life as tested by long experience and
confirmed in the success of many generations.   In this
curriculum the study of the ancient languages has been

prominent as training to the power of subtle analysis;
the mathematics, as strengthening to continuity and
rigor of attention, to sharp and bold discrimination;
physics, to give power over nature,—real power, as we
wield and apply her forces, and intellectual, as we in-
terpret her secrets, predict her phenomena, enforce her
laws, and re-create her universe; psychology, that we
may know ourselves and so understand the instrument
by which we know at all; ethics, that we may rightly
direct the springs of action and subject the individual
will to the consecrating law of duty; political science,
that we may know the state as to the grounds and limits
of its authority; the science of religion, that we may
justify our faith to the disciplined and instructed reason; history, that we may trace the development of
man and the moral purposes of God; logic, rhetoric,
and literature, that the powers thus enriched and thus
trained may express themselves aptly and skillfully by
writing and in speech.

When we say this curriculum has been prescribed, we
do not mean that the student has been forbidden to
pursue other studies, nor that his time has been so entirely occupied and engrossed by the regular course as
to leave no opportunity for favorite pursuits or general
culture.   On the contrary, the college course has usually
contemplated much additional labor and study, and has
encouraged such efforts and indirectly rewarded them
by special prizes and honors.

Whether or not academic degrees signify little or
much, whether they are of greater value or less, it is
clear that they are sought for, and are likely to be in
the future, and that they ought, therefore, to signify

something. The something which they should signify
is the having pursued with more or less fidelity and
success those branches of study which are essential to
liberal culture.

We do not observe that those who depreciate the
meaning and worth of the degree of Bachelor of Arts
are any the less anxious or determined that the courses
of study which they would substitute shall entitle to
this degree, nor are they less affluent in inventing a
variety of subordinate and special degrees for briefer
and less comprehensive courses of study. The two letters B. A. are certainly as significant as B. S., D. S.,
Ph. B., C. E., M. E., if they are not as valuable.

A strong pressure is just now applied to induce the
colleges to abandon both the theory and the practice of
insisting on a prescribed course of study. Some are
very urgent that students should be freely admitted to
the instructions of the college in any single branch, provided they are qualified to receive such instruction, even
though they may be unable or disinclined to pursue the
other studies that are required for a degree. Others insist that no course of study should be prescribed as the
condition for any academic honor, but that instruction
should be freely dispensed to all who are qualified to
appropriate it ; examinations being held as a test of
progress and acquisition in the departments selected.
Others contend that several parallel courses of study
should be assigned, at the completion of any of which
the student should receive the same or a different degree. Others propose that the course should in part be
prescribed and in part be elective, so that within the
limits assigned the pupil may freely select the studies

5

which may please him best, and on passing his examinations shall receive the common degree.

It is contended by the advocates of these several propositions that in these ways we can exalt the college into a university and invest it with the dignity, the privileges, and, above all, with the freedom, which are supposed to belong to an institution with the more high sounding name.   All these projects do indeed propose to attach to the college some of the features which properly belong to the university, viz. : freedom of election, the gratification of special preferences and tastes, real or supposed, and a direct preparation for the student's contemplated profession or business in life.   But they all fail to provide or require the feature which gives the university its dignity and invests its name with special honor, and that is a *thorough discipline previously undergone and a liberal culture already attained.* These are indispensable before the student is fit to exercise the freedom, to use the selection, or appreciate the instructions which belong to the university.   A university consisting of uncultured and undisciplined youths, whose conceit may be supposed to be in direct proportion to their ignorance, and whose self-confidence springs out of their lack of knowledge, is the less to be desired for the highest ends of a university exactly in proportion to the amplitude of its endowments, the brilliancy and learning of its professors, and the sanguine hopefulness of its numerous friends.   Its theory is false and its fruits must be disappointing.   It can only become what it calls itself when it shall have developed within itself a college or school of liberal arts which shall train fit pupils for its university classes, and when it shall have employed in its several schools the curricula and methods which are suitable to each.

We grant that it may be desirable to establish institutions in the large cities and in the newer portions of our country, on the principle of teaching a little of everything that those students may wish to study whose elementary education is deficient and whose time of attendance on either liberal or professional studies must be short. A little knowledge and a little study may be of the greatest service to persons eager to learn. Large endowments, distinguished professors, ample museums, and abundant apparatus may serve to quicken the intellects and to stimulate the zeal of the strong-minded and strong-hearted young men to whom poverty, early toil, or misfortune have abridged the period of school and college culture. The colleges in the newer States, which have a small number of students in their regular course, have acted wisely and beneficently in allowing the attendance of irregular and optional pupils, so far as this did not interfere with the efficiency and prestige of the liberal curriculum. What we do not approve, is the dignifying of institutions of any kind with the name of universities, when they lack the one feature which gives to the university all its dignity and peculiar meaning, and that is the presence of a considerable body of students of liberal culture who are prepared by that culture to select some higher department of knowledge and to pursue it under the teachers of their choice, by free and independent methods of study. For example: The Michigan University has been more than once especially extolled as till recently the only real university in the United States, and no measured laudation has on this account been bestowed upon the institution and the enterprising State which endowed it. This has been done by gentlemen of eminent literary culture and of high position in older institutions. We have never been able to learn any reason for these encomiums upon this institution, nor why it is *par éminence* a university in comparison with Harvard, except that while it furnishes a considerable number of well qualified professors in many departments of knowledge, the students are permitted to some extent to attend upon more or fewer of these courses at will, without the condition of previous training in the liberal arts. Other institutions claim that as compared with this relatively conservative university they are entitled to be called universities *sensu eminentiori*, because they impose only the most general conditions and regulations with respect to previous preparation or the choice of the departments to be studied. They argue, in effect, that is indeed *a university* which teaches universal knowledge universally—*i. e.*, to all comers—in which no man shall be denied who asks to be taught anything. But this feature, so far from elevating into a university what might have been a college, tends to degrade what might be a college into a preparatory school, and even to sink it to the level of those most superficial but most pretentious things called "business or commercial colleges." The ineffable assurance and the contemptible performance of these peripatetic and short-lived organizations are sufficiently notorious.

It ought, as it would seem, to be an axiom in education that, to successful instruction, the capacity of the school to receive is as essential as the power of the instructor to give. Pupils capable of understanding and appropriating what is taught are as necessary as instructors who are qualified to teach. Eminent professors may indeed astonish the beginner by the splendor of their generalizations, the boldness of their theories, the eloquence of their delivery, or the perfection of their style. They may quicken and stimulate to industry and ardor. But unless their hearers or pupils are already educated to the capacity of understanding and appreciating their teachings, they must be content to be ranked with the brilliant sciolist and the splendid declaimer, even in the judgment of their scholastic audiences, and in the judgment of the public to rank as somewhat lower, or, perhaps, at best, to serve as imposing figure heads to badly trimmed and badly sailing vessels. Such men cannot but be useful indeed, for they will insensibly diffuse the spirit and impart the tone of a higher scholarship and culture to not a few of the raw and uncultured pupils who come within their reach. But the partial success of gifted and learned professors, in spite of the defective theory of the institutions with which they are connected, only serves the more strikingly to illustrate the essential defects of the system itself.

The modification of the college system, which we shall next consider, is that which does not abandon a prescribed curriculum, but makes the college studies *largely elective*. This does not sacrifice the college to the university system. It rather combines the one with the other, by introducing some of the features of the university into the system of the college. It requires all the students to pursue a common course up to a certain period. At Harvard College, this continues to the end of the Freshman year ; a selection is then allowed, till the end of the course, of any two or three of certain studies, for about two-thirds of the time, the remaining third being devoted to certain studies pursued by the class in common. Prominent among these elective studies are the ancient languages and the mathematics, to the end of the course. The arguments urged in favor of this system are these. While it requires all the students to master the elements of liberal knowledge, it does not require that any one study should be pursued to such an extreme as to weary those to whom it is distasteful, or to take the place of studies for which there is a marked predilection or special aptitude. It furnishes the opportunity to the student to make a selection with some reference to his future occupation or profession. It adopts the happy medium of insisting on the necessity of a common groundwork of preparation in disciplinary studies, and providing for each an election as the tastes and pursuits of the pupil may require. It satisfies the devotee of any special department of knowledge by allowing him to follow his favorite studies. It excites him by the emulation and sympathy of fellow students as eager to learn and as ready to labor as himself. It releases the instructor from the intolerable and disgusting drudgery of enforcing upon the unwilling and incompetent, tasks which they cannot or will not perform, and gratifies him with the pleasure of carrying a few enthusiastic pupils far beyond the elements of the language or science to which he himself is devoted. It tends to enthusiasm in study and is fitted to relieve the college system from the spirit of mechanical routine into which it is so apt to fall.

The objections to the scheme are many; some of them seem to us to be insuperable. They may be expressed briefly thus : The collegiate course will be so seriously shortened and curtailed as to fail of its appropriate results ; the university course, which it is proposed to graft upon it, will be prematurely commenced, and, for that reason, cannot be really successful. College students, at the end of the Freshman year, are usually incapable of selecting between any two proposed studies or courses of study. They do not know themselves well enough to be able to decide in what they are best fitted to excel, nor even what will please them best. Their future occupation is ordinarily not so far determined as to deserve to be seriously considered. Their tastes are either unformed or capricious and prejudiced ; if they are decided and strong, they often require correction. The study which is the farthest removed from that which strikes his fancy may be the study which is most needed for the student. The preferences are also likely to be fickle. The real but unanticipated difficulties which are revealed by trial will occasion discontent and vexation, or some new discovery concerning the value of a study that has been rejected, will lead to ennui and discontent. So far as the studies presented for selection are disciplinary, the reasons for preferring one above another are not so decisive as to warrant any great liberty of election. So far as they are professional or practical, it is not desirable that these should be entered upon at so early a period of the education. What might seem to be gained in proficiency or in time, is lost many times over in mental breadth and power by a neglect of the studies which are disciplinary and general. The student who begins the study of theology or law in his Sophomore or Junior year, or pursues a course of reading which has special relation to his future profession, in ninety out of a hundred instances becomes a greatly inferior theologian or lawyer in consequence, and does not appreciably abridge the time required for his professional preparation. By a similar rule, any very special attention to any one of the physical sciences in the way of severe scientific study or of time-consuming occupation, is almost certain to involve a loss in scientific acquisitions and eminence at the end of a very few years. The speciality or profession to which a student is to give the best energies and the exclusive devotion of his life, will occupy him soon enough at the latest, and will confine his powers as well as rule his tastes with its absorbing demands. All that he can spare from it in the way of energy, preferences, and time, is, in a certain sense, so much gained to his mental breadth, and, therefore, to his final eminence. If it can be shown that there is any single course of study which is within the capacities of the majority of students who are properly prepared and who will use ordinary diligence ; which includes no branch of knowledge with which any man of liberal education ought not to be acquainted ; and if also these branches are not prosecuted farther than is desirable for the ends of such culture ; it follows that such a course of study should be prescribed in every college. This is especially true if it can also be shown that a prescribed course can be so modified as to attain many if not all the advantages which the elective course promises to achieve.

Other objections might be named, as that the intro-duction of elective studies tends to weaken the class feeling, which may be so efficient for intellectual incite-ment and culture, and to interfere with that common life which is so powerful in most of the American col-leges. It must necessarily be complicated in its ar-rangements and operose in its working. It must also require greater energy than can be exacted of any sin-gle administrator who acts as the driving wheel of the class or the college ; or greater united and conspiring activity in the heads of separate departments than can be presumed in ordinary institutions or under the con-ditions of our imperfect humanity. It may further be urged that the existence of a prescribed, rather than an elective curriculum in the preparatory or the profes-sional school, was originally the result of circumstan-ces and the product of experience. The same circum-stances that compelled and the same experience which taught it at first, will, we believe, require that it be re-sumed as often as the attempt is made to abandon it in any institution which is designed for general culture. The inconvenience will be found to be so great and the advantages so inconsiderable—if, indeed, the disadvan-tages are not so manifold and overwhelming—as to compel a return to what is substantially a uniform and prescribed course. We have intimated that most of the advantages promised by the elective, may be secured by the prescribed curriculum. It does not follow because the same branches of study are pursued that they must be prosecuted by all the students to the same extent or with the same thoroughness. A minimum of classical study may be allowed, while a maximum may be rewarded. A passable knowledge of the mathematics may be accepted, while a more thorough mastery of these branches may meet with encouragement and the more difficult problems need be assigned to but few. An arrangement or curriculum of *pass studies* prescribed for all, which shall be thorough and severe, is not incompatible with provision for *class or honor studies*, which shall be the conditions of academical prizes and distinctions. Private studies may also be provided for, to a limited extent, especially in those branches of literature, English or modern, which are the favorite and not severe occupation of many persons who are not inclined to the severer efforts required by philosophy or science. The division of classes into subordinate sections, according to attainment, provides for a varying adaptation to different tastes and capacities. Enthusiasm in study, the want of which is so much to be deplored, and the maintenance of a high intellectual tone, the presence of which is so greatly to be desired, can be obtained, we believe, as successfully under the prescribed as under the elective curriculum.

We have said that in almost every organized institution of education in the civilized world, whether liberal or professional, some curriculum of study is presented as the condition of receiving the honors of the institution, or of being admitted to public employment. The fact that several such courses are united in the same institution makes it to be a university, which is therefore properly conceived when it embraces a collection of schools of learning, in each of which certain studies are prescribed, certain terms must be kept, and certain examinations must be passed, before the pupil can receive the certificate or degree which they all contemplate. The fact that in some universities single courses of lectures may be attended by those who expect no certificate or degree, has caused the impression to prevail to some extent in this country, that these exceptions exemplify the rule of university life. Nothing can be more untrue. In the *German universities*, which constitute with many the *beau idéal* of what the American colleges ought to become, the great mass of the students attend the lectures which are necessary in order to qualify them to pass the examination which is required before they are admitted to their life career. It is true, a few persons are admitted to the lectures who do not look forward to an examination, and who attend what lectures they please, but such are not members of the university, except they are from a foreign country. In the theory of university instruction and administration, there is no *option of studies ;* the option is between several *instructors* in the same department of knowledge, and between a faithful and careless use of its opportunities ; the last being no advantage to speak of.

Another point still more material to be considered, and one that is almost universally overlooked in this country, is, that in Germany the gymnasium is the counterpart of the American college. The proposal in America, that the colleges should become universities, is equivalent to the proposal in Germany that the gymnasia should be transformed into universities ; that is, that the instruction now given in two or three advanced classes of the gymnasium should be omitted in whole or in part, in order that the student might be admitted at once to professional or scientific study. Such a

proposition in Germany would be received with derision.   We observe, in passing, that as the gymnasium
answers to the American college, so the *Realschule* correspond to the scientific school with us,—rather, to
the scientific school as it was originally conceived in
this country, for the form which these schools are now
taking, *e. g.*, the Sheffield School and the Massachusetts
Institute of Technology, brings them somewhat nearer
to the gymnasium.   But even when the curriculum of
these schools shall be extended to four years, and Latin
shall be insisted on as a preliminary study, they will
scarcely rise higher in their programme than do the real
schools of Germany.   But these schools, in Germany,
prepare for business or practical life only.   To matricu-
lation and full membership in the university, and to a
certificate or degree founded upon an attendance on the
lectures in physics, the old-fashioned classical course
of the gymnasium is the indispensable prerequisite.   It
is so because the university professes to teach Science
and not Technology, and to scientific knowledge in the
eminent sense, an antecedent preparation of liberal culture is thought to be necessary.   Those Americans who
plead the German universities as models for our colleges, could not, therefore, avail themselves of a more
unfortunate source whence to derive their tirades against
classical study or a prescribed curriculum.   They have
one feature only which can be thus applied ; the student is not held to so strict account as in our colleges
for his attendance upon lectures or for the use of his
time.   The principal motives which hold him to his
duty are the love of study, and the desire for reputation, which are, actively stimulated by a public senti-

ment such as is found in no other country ; and last, not least, by the intimate connection between fidelity in study and his future subsistence, which is so sensitively felt in a country in which the avenues to a decent living are choked by crowds of struggling competitors, and are guarded by numerous artificial barriers. But notwithstanding these stimulants to labor, the success of the German university system is not so remarkable as to justify the confident inferences which are urged by its American encomiasts when they argue that the American college system can only be redeemed by being modeled after its practice. The utmost that Matthew Arnold dares assert to its advantage, is the following : " There are, of course, many idlers ; the proportion of students in a German university who really work, I have heard estimated at one-third ; certainly it is larger than in the English universities." (p. 229.) Mark Pattison asserts of the students at Oxford, that seventy per cent. are " idle, incorrigibly idle." If these estimates are correct, we are confident that defective as are the operation and results of the American colleges, none of them will present so scanty a proportion of earnest and successful workers as do the English and German universities, while our professional and advanced schools, which should more properly be compared with these, would make a much better showing. We speak not of actual attainments, but only of the spirit of labor. How ruinous and demoralizing it would be to allow to the students of the American colleges the freedom and irresponsibility of the German university, a freedom which would not for a moment be thought of in the gymnasium, needs scarcely a moment's thought. Even if the grade of the students in the university and the college were the same, the circumstances of the two countries are so diverse as to exclude all inferences from the one to the other. The influence of a learned class is with us comparatively feeble. The pecuniary prizes offered directly to scholastic attainment are far from being tempting. The road is nearly as direct and open to the professions from the log-cabin as from the university ; to political success it is quite as free and as crowded from the one starting-point as it is from the other. The colleges and schools have nothing of the value in the eye of the " politicians" in America, which the university has in the view of the government in Germany, where all the patronage with respect to the more important civil offices, flows in a stream exclusively through the literary institutions, and is determined by the examinations held by the civil authorities. These, and manifold other circumstances explain the energy and zeal with which science is pursued in the German gymnasia and the German universities. Were their system very diverse from our own, success with them would be no warrant for success with us. But inasmuch as their system is substantially the same with our own in respect to a prescribed course of study, it may confirm us in the purpose not hastily to abandon a feature which has been almost universally accepted, wherever literary institutions have been instructed by the wisdom, or have stood the test, of time.

The results of the experiment of the elective system at Harvard College, as described in the report of the late acting President for 1868–69, are not such as to diminish our confidence in the views which have been expressed. We give this part of the report in full, because of the importance of the subject and the significance of the views it expresses : " The elective system has been in operation long enough to develop both its merits and its defects. It has probably disappointed equally its opponents and its advocates. It has not drained the classical departments of such pupils as would have remained in them with honor and profit ; nor has it lowered the standard of scholarship. It is believed that there is at least as much of good work done under the present as under the former *régime*, and with more alacrity. It is a decided advantage to the working of any department to be relieved of those who dislike it or are unfitted for it. It is impossible that teachers should not do themselves the more ample justice when they have only capable and willing pupils ; and equally impossible that students should not make greater proficiency in such branches as they elect for themselves than in a required course. So far as the election on the part of our students is free, deliberate, and for just cause, these benefits have manifestly attended their choice. But a large portion of the students make their election, not from any conscious taste or preference, but avowedly from considerations of ease, or of rank, or of companionship. As the time for choice approaches, no question is more frequently discussed than the higher or lower rate at which the several instructors estimate equally good lessons ; and a department is not unfrequently chosen because it is supposed, that, in the College phrase, " the marks run higher" there than in the collateral departments. The very large number of petitions for " a change of elective" is the best evidence of the insufficient grounds on which the choice is often made. It must be admitted, also, that the instructors are strongly tempted to do whatever is legitimately within their power to dissuade and discourage all except quick and capable scholars from entering their respective departments ; and a student of slender ability, but with a sincere and discriminating love of learning, may find the course which he would prefer virtually closed against him, or opened to him reluctantly and grudgingly. The undersigned would by no means recommend a return to the old method. The elective system is entitled to a prolonged and thorough trial. It was demanded by the public voice ; it is sustained by the suffrages of many of our wisest and most experienced educators. But, in order to give it a fair and full trial, it should be confined to those who wish to exert the prerogative it gives. It should not be discredited by the haphazard, miscalled choice, which on the first week of a term may crowd one recitation-room with students who, the second week, will be pertinaciously begging to be transferred to another. It is recommended that the present, and, whenever it shall be practicable, a still wider, range of choice be open to all who desire that liberty ; but that there be also established a regular *curriculum*, not unlike the former required course, which shall be pursued by those who signify no wish to do otherwise. This arrangement would restore to the ancient routine of liberal study all who have no special tastes or adaptations, and would at the same time disencumber of indifferent pupils the special departments that have been added to the old *curriculum*."

The opinions and recommendations contained in this extract which are founded upon the actual workings of the elective system should be distinguished from those which are grounded upon other reasons. The wisdom of a regular curriculum for all those who do not desire an election is distinctly recognised. At the same time the frivolous and capricious reasons which excite such a desire in many cases, the unwisdom of the election made, as well as the injurious temptation to which the instructors are exposed to recommend to certain students total abstinence from their class-rooms, are all eminently suggestive. An optional system that could be rigidly restricted to those students and those studies between which there exists an irresistible affinity—if it were subordinated to a regular curriculum which should be rigidly enforced in all cases in which no such reason for election could be made to appear, would be attended with few very serious objections, except that the student himself might in many cases be a serious loser. Under such an arrangement the college would give the weight of its influence in favor of what may properly be called the " well rounded" system of studies as the condition of manly and liberal culture. The force of its discipline, and the pressure of the joint working of every part of its adjusted machinery would all be brought to bear in one direction, and the confident impetuosity of youthful conceit with its restless desire of change would be quietly regulated. We cannot but hope it is in this direction and after this ideal that the words of the sanguine President of Harvard will be fulfilled, which announce that " the college therefore proposes to persevere in its efforts to improve and extend the elective system."

The reasons which introduce the "therefore" in this announcement are not especially convincing, being made up of pleasant and obvious generalities with a slight glitter of specious humor. For example: "The enforced and uniform curriculum has the merit of simplicity. So had the school method of our grandfathers, —one primer, one catechism, one rod for all children." We beg pardon—we had supposed that the "one rod" was electively reserved for those who especially deserved it—and among other reasons for bad logic. Of bad logic or a misapplied analogy the President's next paragraph seems to us an example. The adherence by the Americans to the uniform curriculum is cited as an outgrowth of the tendency of the Yankee to believe that he can turn his hand to anything, *i. e.,* the Yankee colleges have generally confined their students to a fixed course of studies, in the belief that their genius when thus trained would render them dexterous in any special art without further preparation. The observation, " the vulgar conceit that a Yankee can turn his hand to anything we insensibly carry into high places where it is preposterous and criminal," is better illustrated by those directors of public education who think a Yankee student is " roundly " developed at a period so much earlier than he is in England or Germany that it is safe to trust him to choose his own specialty some two or three years sooner than is allowed in those countries. " The young man of nineteen or twenty ought to know what he likes best and is most fit for," says the Yankee President. On the contrary, Lord Macaulay, a rather slow Englishman, observes : " We believe that men who have been engaged up to one or two and twenty, in studies which have no immediate connection with the business of any profession, and of which the effect is merely to open, to invigorate, and to strengthen the mind, will generally be found, in the business of every profession, superior to men who have at eighteen or nineteen devoted themselves to the especial studies of their calling." This opinion is expressed in an elaborate and well considered report founded on an actual observation of the results of a special education for the East India service, a service, success in which demands technical studies in a whole family of difficult languages, in a tangled and doubtful history, and a recondite philosophy and theology. The President says, very truly, " if the previous training" of the young man of nineteen or twenty " has been sufficiently wide he will know by that time whether he is most apt at language, or philosophy, or natural science, or mathematics." " *If*"—but the conclusion all depends on the *if.* Whether this is usually the case is the very, and the only point in dispute. We have as yet no satisfactory evidence that the students of Harvard College at the end of the Freshman year have attained to more advanced acquisitions of knowledge as well as to greater maturity of mind, than is granted to youths in general at this stage of college life. Perhaps it is the expectation that the college can enforce so thorough a classical and mathematical training upon applicants for admission as to be able to terminate the strictly disciplinary course of required studies at the end of Freshman year. If this is so, it would seem to be preferable that a system of special schools—say of Philology, Philosophy, History, Literature, etc., etc.—should be provided, each with its fixed curriculum. This would involve a *shortening* of the time allotted to both liberal and special education, and this would illustrate another peculiarity sometimes charged upon " the Yankees"— that they shorten the time required for long and deliberate work. This shortening or condensing process must involve the curtailing of the Latin and Greek, an effect which is open to the objection, made by an acute friend of ours, that it seems hardly worth while to commence the study of either Latin or Greek if either or both of these languages are to be prosecuted no further than is provided at Harvard. It certainly would illustrate still another American peculiarity, the being content with a *smattering* in studies.

It may perhaps be the design at Harvard to absorb the Scientific School into the college, and after the Freshman year to give to modern languages, history and literature, natural history, etc., the time which has hitherto been devoted to the severer occupations, on the theory that the disciplinary and professional studies can be advantageously combined in the college course. Our whole argument has been directed against such a plan and the reasons which we have adduced are not set aside by the remark of the President, that all the studies open to the student " are liberal and disciplinary, not narrow and special" ; and again, the requisitions for the first degree " are nevertheless high and inflexible, being nothing less than four years devoted to liberal culture." Doubtless all these studies are disciplinary. That has never been questioned and hardly needed to have been reaffirmed. The question in discussion is, not whether these " modern" and special studies are disciplinary in any degree, but whether they are *as* eminently disciplinary as those for which they are substituted. Or is it desired to transform the college into a continental university as modified by the Yankee device of admitting young students to the election and the freedom of the university, without that previous discipline or knowledge which is requisite for success? Harvard has had for a long time the name of a university, with very much of the reality, in that one of its departments which has followed the methods hitherto characteristic of the college. It would be a public loss and a pity if she should cease to be a college, and fail to be any thing more than the mere semblance of a university. We venture to predict that if the new system is persevered in, Harvard College will contain three or four sets of students among its undergraduates : 1st. The devotees of classical learning or of mathematical research, who, in their "small and lively classes" and with the aid of accomplished and earnest teachers, will prosecute their studies with excited enthusiasm and make brilliant acquisitions ; 2d. The devotees of some special branch of Physical Science who will pursue their studies either from the excitement of love, or the interest which is derived from their intimate relation to future professional success ; 3d. A higher class than either, viz. : those who by reason of early youthful advantages or precocious genius have the capacity and taste for properly university studies, a great number of which they will select and master ; 4th. A large, inferior, and heterogeneous class, who will select their "electives" with the keenest appreciation of what will yield a living standing at the least expense of labor —camp-followers and stragglers, who will require a vigorous Provost Marshal to look after and to connect them in reputable relations with the principal battalions. The connection between these several divisions must be loose and uninteresting, the sense of interest in, and responsibility for, the institution as a whole must be weak in the instructors, the common life of the college must be relaxed and feeble in its tone, and the degree with which all the members of these ill assorted classes are to be honored at the close must signify a frightful inequality of opportunities enjoyed, if not of acquisitions actually made. That Harvard College will continue to be an institution of great activity and acquisition in all departments of learning and culture, cannot be doubted ; but that Harvard College will be as useful to the public and to many of its students, as it would be if its awakening enterprise and its great resources had been administered on a different theory, we may be excused from believing, without abating in the least our sympathy with the enterprise or our personal respect for the honest intentions and public spirit of its guardians—least of all, without diminishing our estimate of the learning and genius of its eminent instructors.

IV.

TEXT BOOKS AND LECTURES.

Another marked peculiarity of the American colleges is the frequent examinations of the students, or *the recitations*, as they are called. This feature is almost unknown in the English universities ; the examinations occurring occasionally in the colleges for standing and prizes, say two or three times a year, and more rarely in the university—at " the Senate House" or in " the Schools"—for university degrees and for the great rewards that bring fellowships and livings. In the German gymnasia it is rigidly maintained, modified, indeed, by the German methods of giving instruction. In the German universities frequent examinations are altogether unknown. After the student has passed through the final examination in the gymnasium, which answers to our Bachelor's degree, he is free of all intermeddling except the stern arbitrament which awaits him from the government officials who give him his passport to place and position in life, or the more trying one from the Senatus Academicus which shall promote him to a Doctor's hat. In the Scotch universities the examinations are more or less frequent, according to the subject matter, but the instruction is given in large measure by lectures and the final examinations are conducted by the representatives of the professions, for the license to practice in the guild or the church. In the Queen's Colleges and the London University there are examinations for degrees and honors, and more or less frequent examinations to ascertain the proficiency and to stimulate the activity of the student. The German gymnasium and the American college insist on these very frequent daily examinations or recitations. Instruction is not excluded from these exercises. It is imparted more or less freely according to the knowledge and skill of the instructor and the receptivity of his pupils, but the prominent feature is the examination of the student's private work for the purpose of holding him to his daily duties by a constant and even pressure of responsibility, and of noticing and measuring his attainments under the watchful eye of his tutor and the not uninterested inspection of his fellows. For the sake of making this responsibility more effective and just, the practice has been introduced into many colleges of recording the work of every recitation by a mark according to a numerical scale. These daily examinations are, in most of the colleges, supplemented by examinations at the end of every term and of every year, and in some by a final examination upon the whole of the course, for the Bachelor's degree. In many the examinations at the end of one or of two years serve, so far, as the final trial for the degree.

In connection with these recitations from a text-book, lectures are given in greater or less number—*i. e.* oral expositions and enforcements of facts or truths—with experiments in the case of the physical sciences, and other illustrations in history, literature, and philosophy. Upon these lectures examinations are usually held. In

a few of the colleges, instruction is given very largely
by lectures, and great reliance is placed upon the examinations held upon the lectures heard, in comparison
with recitations from text-books. In others, text-books
are made the chief instruments or occasions of oral instruction. The methods of conducting these recitations
vary very greatly in different institutions, according to
the traditions of the college, the number of the students, the knowledge and skill, the fidelity and affable-
ness of the instructors.

It is, of course, implied, and ought here to be noticed, that attendance upon these recitations and lectures is required, and that in some colleges the custom
has been introduced of also exacting that the lesson
should be recited privately in every case in which an
absence has been excused, certain exceptions being allowed for long illness, and other reasons ; if the absence is not excused or the lesson is not recited, the
student suffers in his standing.

We have named all these features together, because
they are features of a common system and because every
one of them has been of late much discussed. They
do not necessarily go together, but they are all special applications of a common principle of college administration, viz., the principle of frequent and enforced examinations. The principle itself we are prepared to
defend as essential to the successful administration of
the American college, and indeed to all thorough education in such a country as ours. The special modes
of applying and enforcing it are all the fruits of experience, and are not only capable of being vindicated as
defensible, but may be recommended as important im-

6

provements. We will consider these features in order. We notice, first of all, the relative advantages and disadvantages of giving instruction by *text-books and lectures*. This point has been very earnestly discussed in this country. Not a few contend that the only method of instruction which is becoming the dignity of a scholar, is instruction by lectures. For an eminent philologist or scientist to do anything but give prelections upon his science, is represented as a profound degradation. It is held by many that the college, if it aims to be a university, should furnish instruction in no other form, and leave the students to be attracted and held to the lecture-room by the ability, reputation, or eloquence of the professor ; subject only to occasional examinations upon the knowledge which they have acquired, and their fitness to enter into certain employments. These views have been propounded in this country for the past thirty years with great earnestness and zeal. Scarcely a day elapses in which some writer in a newspaper or journal does not take up and repeat the refrain. Inasmuch as lectures upon certain branches of physics seem to be required in order to exhibit experiments by apparatus, the professors of these branches and their friends are foremost in insisting that oral exposition by lecture is the only method of teaching which ought to be required by the institution or submitted to by the professor. In some institutions in this country, particularly in the University of Virginia, it is used very generally in all departments of knowledge. This is the only method practiced in the German universities with some very limited exceptions. In the great English universities it is used but little, and meets with scanty favor. In the Scotch universities it is largely used, as it is also in the Queen's Colleges, and we believe in the colleges of the London University.

Instruction by lectures is the most attractive to the teacher, especially if he consults his private ease, comfort, and reputation more than he considers his usefulness or effectiveness as a teacher, or the best interests of the institution which he serves. This is especially true if the professor is required to give one or two courses of some thirty or fifty hours a year, and if with the preparation and delivery of these lectures his responsibility begins and ends. Even when he lectures an hour every day, or even more frequently, it is an immense relief to know that he has no concern with the progress and fidelity of the students, except to give them sound and methodical teaching. Lecturing is especially attractive when a man can be appointed to a special lectureship in one or more universities, and receive a handsome stipend for reading ten or twenty prelections upon a subject to which he is supposed to have given special attention. A Professorship limited to such duties is, moreover, a very convenient endowment for the devotee of any special department of knowledge ; giving him position in connection with an influential and learned community, a limited excitement in the obligation to deliver a few lectures yearly, which may sustain his reputation and make public his discoveries, and leisure for private studies, for the enlargement of science, and the honor of the university. But however attractive this method of instruction may be, in its relations to the dignity, the ease, the irresponsibility, or the pocket of the instructor, or even to the enlargement

and defense of science, it is not the most profitable to
the pupil, unless he is far advanced in knowledge and
is animated with an ardent zeal for learning. Even
then it has only a limited usefulness and should never
be exclusively employed. Its advantages, when used
within proper limits, are the following : The instruction
is given from a living man, with the interest and excitement which personal presence and oral communication
possess above the written page. The accessories of an
audience, composed of others intent upon the same
themes, and moved by the same activities of thought
and feeling, are not inconsiderable. The methodizing
agency of an able thinker in recasting and representing
acknowledged principles and received facts in such relations as are peculiar to himself, with especial reference to the known wants of his hearers, to current objections, to prevailing controversies, and to popular
literature or passing events, whether public or private,
is of the greatest importance. The Professor has been
constituted and accepted by his class as their teacher,
and communications from him are received with a def-
erence and trust which are accorded to no other person.
It is often difficult, sometimes it is impossible, for him
to find a manual or text-book which accords with his
opinions or method. For this reason, even if he uses
a text-book, he must lecture more or less, in order to
supply its deficiencies or rearrange its method. Even
when he relies chiefly upon a text-book and recitations,
lectures may be required to present matter which can
only be gathered from many authorities, which the student is incapable of looking up and arranging for himself, but which, when presented in connection with the

author recited, invests the study of the subject with a heightened interest, and impresses its truths more firmly upon the memory. A brief course of lectures is often of the greatest importance as a means of gathering together what has been read or studied, of restating it in a compact and intelligible method, and impressing it more firmly upon the memory. Lectures, also, help to reveal the individual peculiarities of the Professor's intellect and heart more fully, and in more particulars, than his occasional comments upon the authors which are recited, because the discussions can be more complete and exhaustive. They are of special importance in case the teacher has made important discoveries, or seized upon important truths, or invented a new method, or completed a peculiar system. The necessity and usefulness of lectures for these and other ends, will, however, vary very considerably with different studies and departments. Instruction in the Mathematics and in the Classics, with the exception of special topics of History and Antiquities, can be most advantageously given in connection with a text-book upon which the Professor comments and the pupil is examined.

The objections to an exclusive reliance upon lectures for instruction in any department of college teaching are manifold. The pupil receives by the ear and not by the eye. The eye can re-peruse what it sees and can reflect upon its import. The ear must hear it a second time, either as repeated, or as given in varied phraseology, and made obvious and palpable by copious illustrations. Hence the lecturer must necessarily be slow and tedious, or diffuse, repetitious, or superficial. Hence if a pupil relies upon a lecturer for all the knowledge which he acquires, his acquisitions will be scanty and imperfectly grounded, even if he employs his own thinking in revising and recasting what he has heard. A remembered lecture is vastly inferior to a thoroughly mastered book, because the book will ordinarily be more condensed and scientific than the lecture, or, if not, more of it will be retained and placed methodically at the service of the learner The reason why lectures are especially adapted to students who have read and mastered many books, is that the teacher in such cases may revise and recast the knowledge which they have acquired, or, if it need be, supply what is wanting or confute what is erroneous, and have an audience intelligent and appreciative by reason of their previously acquired knowledge.

Not only can the pupil gain less positive knowledge and fewer thoughts from a lecture than from an hour's reading, and for this reason receive less advantage, but he will acquire this knowledge in a manner which will less vigorously exercise and discipline his powers. The fact that acquisition by the lecture is the most pleasant, may indicate that the attitude of the pupil is passive and receptive rather than active and recreative. The stimulus and aid furnished by the presence and voice of the teacher may be at the expense of the self-exciting and self-controlled activity of the learner. Attendance upon lectures is exhaustive of the body and the mind, and it is especially injurious to both the taste and the power for close and effective private study. If the chief reliance is placed upon lectures, five or six hours of close attention will constitute sufficient labor for the day, and the remainder of the time of the pupil must be given to studying his notes for retention or examination. The consequence will be that very little reading will be accomplished and the student will become the passive recipient of the doctrines and opinions of his teachers, and hence, even under the ablest and most various instruction, narrow in his range of knowledge and of thought, if not the passionate and bigoted adherent of a single school, with few resources and a feebler inclination to correct his defects.

For the more advanced students of a college, and even for the students of professional schools, instruction by lecturing should be sparingly applied. It should never supersede the independent reading of the student nor the task-work of individual acquisition and thought. For pupils who are less advanced it should be employed very rarely, and only for the purposes of rousing the attention, stimulating the zeal, and gathering into brief and comprehensive statements the most general views of the topic or author which is studied. The chief occupation of such students should be to commit to memory, and to master by thought, the words and principles which the text-books present for study. The use of a text-book is, however, in no sense degrading to the instructor, nor does it preclude him from giving instruction in the amplest variety and the most effective manner. The teacher is not necessarily degraded to the position of a mere examiner of his pupils' work or a hearer of recitations. On the contrary, he enjoys special advantages for the most effective teaching, viz., teaching by the Socratic method. The defects of his author in statement or in method may even be the convenient occasion and foil to set off his own better phrased definitions or his neater methods. The felicitous or defective performance of his pupil may excite the instructor to draw forth the vindication or the correction of his work by well adapted questionings. Instruction given in this way is more concrete and lively than the more general and abstract expositions of the lecture-room. To comment upon an author may task the powers and display the genius of the most gifted teacher as effectively and variously as to utter his own lucubrations. Indeed the brief foot-notes of a learned commentator upon a printed text are often as valuable as the learned dissertations which he reserves for the appendix. Instruction by this method has also the very great advantage of bringing the teacher into a close and individual contact with his pupil, of giving him a personal knowledge of his powers and his defects, and sometimes of awakening an humane and friendly interest in his progress. The familiar questionings of the class-room open and invite the way to profitable intercourse and acquaintance in private. They tend to bring both pupil and teacher into the relations of confidence and friendship, and thus to make real the ideal of friendly guidance on the one hand and of grateful docility on the other.

We dwell upon this point at greater length, for the reason that the opinion has extensively prevailed in this country, and is countenanced by manifold influences, that the American colleges can never rise to their proper position until they are manned by a large number of eminent professors, to each of whom shall be assigned a lecture-room for instruction, and whose sole function shall be to read or expound the results of his

individual researches. If examinations are to be enforced, it is held that even these should be conducted
by assistants or tutors, but from 'all duties of this sort
which involve a close personal knowledge of and interest in the progress of the individual pupil the professor
should seek to be excused, as inconsistent with his position and interfering with his private studies. No heresy
seems to us more dangerous than this. No disaster
could be more serious than for college instructors or
college guardians to cherish such ideals as this of what
is desirable for the college or attainable by a professor.
All tendencies in this direction should be discouraged
as injurious to the welfare of these most important institutions by weakening their efficiency, and as inconsistent with efficient teaching by the instructor and
thorough acquisition by the student.

If a man desires to be a professor in an American
college he desires a good work, but he ought to have
just conceptions of the nature of the work which he desires. His official business is to educate the young, *i. e.*,
it is to teach and to train. This is the work for which
the college exists, and for carrying forward which all its
instructors, the professor included, are appointed. It is
true, that in order to teach he must know, and in order
to make progress in knowledge, must continue to study
and learn. In order to continue to learn he must also
have leisure and opportunities. For these reasons he
should not be overworked in teaching ; he should not
be employed so many hours in instruction as to be unable to study with freshness and success, nor, we may
add, should he be so distracted with cares by reason of
insufficient pay, nor so worn with other labors required

by the necessity of earning his living, as to have little strength either for study or instruction. But it should never be forgotten that his post is one of duty to his pupils as an instructor. The American college is not designed primarily to promote the cause of science by endowing posts in which men of learning and science may prosecute their researches, but to secure successful instruction for our youth. In achieving the last object, it incidentally promotes the first, and cannot do otherwise, but its aims should be primarily and distinctly directed to effective instruction as the chief end of its existence. It may be desirable, under certain circumstances, to connect with a college special lectureships to be occupied by distinguished scholars whose duties should be limited. We will not discuss this question here, but would only remark in passing that, whatever the functions of such lecturers may be, they are very subordinate and inconsiderable, compared with those of the instructors who have the charge of classes as their regular employment and devote themselves to the business of education as their principal occupation.

We return to our subject. We assert that it is not only undesirable that our colleges should very largely give instruction by lectures, but that, on the other hand, our more advanced schools of knowledge, both professional and general, would gain in thoroughness and efficiency if they combined with lecturing thorough courses of reading. Nothing is more unsatisfactory in the judgment of one who sees beneath the surface, than the superficial habits and the narrow culture which are contracted by the students of those professional schools in which the instruction is given chiefly by lectures. We

observe hopeful tendencies in these schools toward reform in this very particular, notwithstanding the prevalence of the notion in our speech-making and speech-
admiring country that the millennium of colleges will
never come till they are advanced to universities, and
that to the conception of a university the essential
elements are a library, museums, a suite of lecture-
rooms with a professor in every chair,and classes of
persons with pens and paper, who pay their fees with
regularity and promptness !

But here we shall be met with the familiar inquiries
and objections, how is it with the German Universities?
Is not their practice directly opposed to your theory?
Is not the instruction in these universities given almost
exclusively by lectures? Where in all the world is instruction more valuable or received by a larger number
of appreciative and zealous hearers? To this we reply,
the German Universities, as has already been said, presuppose the Gymnasia. In the education which they
give, both as to matter and form, they adapt themselves
to students who have been trained, in these lower institutions, to the power to understand, to assimilate and
delight in, the lectures which the university gives.
Take away the gymnasia and the hearers who have
been trained by their peculiar method, and the university lecturers would either become unintelligible or else
unprofitable by reason of the incapacity or inadequate
culture of their hearers. The hearers of the university
lectures are also stimulated to attention and zeal by
manifold influences which either do not exist, or act but
feebly in this country. Nor is it true, as is often represented, that the majority of the hearers of these lec-

tures are either enthusiastic or eminently successful devotees of knowledge. The enthusiasm of a few, upon subjects which excite in this country the ardor of only here and there a solitary devotee, is indeed most noticeable, but this is not in the least to be ascribed to the fact that the instruction is given by lectures. This enthusiasm is more frequent and more fervent, as not a few attendants upon the universities have had occasion to notice, at those exercises in which the instruction is given more nearly after the English and American methods. A large number of the students are negligent and idle, though they have been trained by the rigid and persistent discipline of the gymnasia, and though they are stimulated to effort by the manifold excitements of German society,—a larger number than in the American colleges; notwithstanding the prevalent impression in this country to the contrary. Last of all, the judgment of many of the most intelligent professors and educators in Germany itself is in favor of modifying the lecture system by introducing instruction by recitations to a large extent. The only insuperable obstacle which these opinions encounter is the indolence and indisposition of the professors themselves, who greatly prefer a system which relieves them of the drudgery and petty details which the other method seems to involve.

The authority of the example of the great English universities is decidedly against instruction by lectures. The few lecturers who are provided are little esteemed and scantily attended on. Now and then a brilliant and able professor attracts a few scores of admiring listeners, but the educating influence of his instructions is very inconsiderable. Of late a reforming party has sprung up within and without the universities, who argue from the eminent scholarship and the scientific zeal which prevails in the German universities, that if a system similar to theirs were introduced in England it would be followed by similar zeal and proficiency. In these judgments they overlook or underestimate the very admirable results which the English method, objectionable and deficient as it is in the particulars complained of, has effected in the manhood and power of the multitudes of its reading men. They also entirely leave out of view the difference in the structure of English and German society and in the motives which in the two countries stimulate to intellectual activity, as well as determine the directions in which this activity shall be employed.

V.

THE ENFORCEMENT OF FIDELITY.

Leaving the question between lectures and recitations, we proceed to another point : the *frequency* of the recitations and the manner in which fidelity should be enforced. Should these exercises be frequent or only occasional? Should the acquisitions and diligence of the pupil be estimated daily, or oftener ; or should this be done only at what are technically called examinations, at longer or shorter intervals? We call the attention of our readers to the fact that examinations are required under almost every system and in institutions of all kinds, in the English and German universities, the American colleges, and in most professional and scientific schools. The only difference of opinion concerns the question whether these examinations shall be held rarely and for the single purpose of testing the permanent acquisitions of the student, or whether in addition to such examinations, others shall be held, and very frequently, for the joint purpose of giving instruction and of testing the student's diligence and progress. It should also be noticed that, in all institutions, marks or their equivalents are employed at what are technically called examinations, and that the only difference of opinion relates to the question whether they shall be also employed in what are technically called recitations. In the English universities the private tutor, or *coach*, hears the pupil recite his classics and his mathematics, but he does this simply to prepare him for his examination, whether this be a class or a pass examination. He hears him recite while he works with him—oftener while he works at him—for the purpose of correcting his errors, of inculcating what he needs to notice and remember, and above all, that he may quicken and strengthen his capacity to retain and recall what he learns. In the great schools of England the practice of daily recitations is as abundantly insisted on as it is in the American schools and colleges ; the manner of conducting them being determined by the kind of work which the pupil is required to furnish. In the German gymnasia the pupils perform more of their studying in the presence and by the aid of the teacher than with us. Dictations are abundant, which the pupil records as they fall from the lips of the instructor. Passages in the classics are read and commented on by the teacher ; the principles and examples in mathematics are expounded and explained before the classes. The five hours of attendance are indeed more conspicuously hours of instruction and of acquisition, of joint and excited labor on the part of instructor and pupil, than they are in the English public schools and in the American colleges. But the pupil also recites, and his task ordinarily is not complete without a great deal of work out of school, the results of which he brings up for the satisfaction of the teacher. Whatever is set as a task or has been communicated in the class-room is reproduced by the scholar and may be called for at any time.

In the American colleges the practice has till recently been uniform. Very frequent recitations have been required and the performance of the student at every one of these exercises has been estimated in determining his scholarship, whether or not an entry was made by marks. Formerly the examinations were more hurried and superficial than they should have been. They were usually *viva voce;* written answers from a series of questions being comparatively unknown. Of late, marks have been introduced at the daily as well as at the occasional examinations, and the occasional examinations have been far more formal and thorough. Indeed in respect of form and thoroughness, though not in respect of quality or quantity of matter, these occasional examinations, both written and *viva voce,* in the best colleges, will compare very favorably with those of such institutions as make occasional examinations the only tests of scholarships and the only grounds for honors. Moreover, till of late the minute attention and the constant pressure applied in the regular recitations, in the form of marks or otherwise, have been intensified in the same degree with the increased breadth and pressure employed in the occasional examinations.

Some tendencies to change have, however, of late been manifest. In one college a great excitement was recently occasioned by the application of marks to recitations evaded by unexcused absence. In connection with this the custom of using marks at all has been complained of as degrading to the manly spirit of the pupils, and this complaint has been reëchoed in not a few of the public journals. The proposal has, in some quarters, almost assumed the form of a demand that marking should be abandoned as savoring too much of the discipline which is fitted for school-boys, and as therefore unsuited to young men at college.   Other objections have been urged, as that it tends to foster the spirit of servile and superficial study, and that it promotes cramming for the recitation immediately impending, as well as brings constantly before the student an immediate gain or loss, one of which he will snatch at and the other he will evade by stealthy and superficial practices, to the damage of his intellectual and personal integrity.   It is objected, moreover, that the attention of the instructor is divided and distracted between the work of instruction and of adjusting the measure of the attainments of his pupils.   For these and other reasons it has been proposed to abandon marking at recitations and even marking for attendance, and to hold somewhat frequent examinations, say whenever an author has been read, or any special topic in science or literature has been finished, which examinations shall be the sole ground of determining the attainments of the pupil and his claims to honors.   In favor of this arrangement it is asserted that the student will study his author and his subject more thoroughly, because he will study not in parts, but as a whole,—that, being thrown somewhat more on his own responsibility, he will study with more manly purposes and a more direct regard to his own self-improvement.   It is claimed, as a chief advantage, that he will "cram" his intellectual nutriment less and digest it more perfectly.

It may be said, on the other hand, that all these advantages may be secured without abandoning the most stringent enforcement of the daily recitations.   Examinations may be multiplied as is proposed, and to any extent, for the purpose of giving the pupil a general view of and command over an author and a subject, and great comparative importance may be attached to such reviews and the student's performances, in the estimate of his scholarship. But the advantages of frequent reviews of this kind need not be purchased by the sacrifice of the advantages which are peculiar to the daily recitations, at which the presence of the pupil is enforced, and his performances are marked. The claim that the substitution of the one for the other as a measure of scholarship would exclude or discourage " cramming," is, in our view, not only wholly untenable, but it suggests the most serious objection against such examinations, when made the sole criterion, that they eminently foster the cramming spirit. Indeed, we do not hesitate to affirm that nothing can intensify this spirit so actively as the introduction of such examinations as a *substitute* for daily enforced recitations. In any school, college, or university, let a single day of the week or the month be devoted to a review and examination upon the work of the week or the month ; and let this be accepted as the chief or only test of that work, and the day or two preceding will inevitably be devoted to the most energetic cramming. The first part of the week or month will, by the less faithful and conscientious be wasted or expended on favorite pursuits, and the work that should have been distributed evenly among the several days will be crowded into one or two. Even the more studious and ambitious will be more careless of their daily studies and of course less qualified to appreciate and assimilate the instruction which is given, and will rely upon their capacity to employ their concentrated energies in reviewing. If it be said that the daily recitations involve a daily cram, we can only reply that a daily cram is less objectionable than a weekly or monthly cram, inasmuch as the quantity taken is smaller and the unnatural strain of the powers is less severe. Moreover, the daily so-called cram renders the strain at the end of the week or month less severe. Indeed it makes the labor less a labor of cramming at all. Superficial, indolent, and unfaithful men will abuse any system, and hence the only question worth considering is, which system grants facilities for the least abuse.

To dispense with the enforced recitation, moreover, would be to throw away one of the chief incidental advantages attained by college discipline, apart from the special culture which it imparts, and that is the training of the man to the power and habit of successfully concentrating and controlling his powers. Such a discipline trains a man to bring his powers to act with their utmost energy, within a given time, to meet an impending necessity. To be able to do this under the varying calls of life with effect, is one great secret of success in any occupation or pursuit. To be able to do this in the greatest diversity of circumstances and exigencies, gives a man the widest and most varied influence. R. W. Emerson says very finely in his "Conduct of Life," that of the conditions of success "the first is the stopping off decisively our miscellaneous activity, and concentrating our force on one or a few points; as the gardener, by severe pruning, forces the sap of the tree into one or two vigorous limbs, instead of suffering it to spindle into a sheaf of twigs." "The one prudence in

life is concentration ; the one evil is dissipation ; and it
makes no difference whether our dissipations are coarse
or fine ; property and its cares, friends, and a social
habit, or politics, or music, or feasting. Everything is
good which takes away one plaything and delusion
more, and drives us home to add one stroke of faithful
work." "Concentration is the secret of strength in
politics, in war, in trade,—in short, in all management
of human affairs. One of the high anecdotes of the
world is the reply of Newton to the inquiry, 'how he
had been able to achieve his discoveries?'—'By always
intending my mind.'" "A man who has that presence
of mind which can bring to him on the instant all he
knows, is worth for action a dozen men who know as
much, but can only bring it to light slowly." The constantly enforced recitations of the college, following
each other day after day, and more than once in the
day, made important as the conditions of success and
honor, and continued for several years, are an admirable discipline to this self-control and self-mastery.
They hold a man to his work by a pressure that he
cannot evade. They train him to bring his powers to
act upon a task that must be achieved within the hour.
They help him to despise slight indispositions, whether
of body or of mind, to set aside inertia and headaches,
to turn from the novel and the newspaper, the gymnasium and the rowing match, in order to meet the demands of the teacher and the class room. If this is
not the way *to treat the pupil as a man*, it is the way *to
make him a man*,—with a man's command over his intellect, and a man's capacity to summon and direct his
energies at will, and to energize them up to the demand

of every occasion. It is because of this very result that
the English university system has done so much for its
reading men, and made out of them the mature, self-
poised, efficient men of action ; and when the occasion
required, men of effective speech. Notwithstanding all
the evils of excessive cramming, increased as they are
by the enormous pecuniary value of the prizes in prospect, notwithstanding, too, the one-sidedness of the curriculum prescribed, the training, simply as training, of
these universities, has done more for England and more
for the world than has ever yet been acknowledged. It
has hardened the bone to a compacter grain, and
toughened the muscle to a finer fibre than any other,
simply because it has aroused and concentrated the energies for the accomplishment of definite tasks, and because, after the training of its champions was complete,
the empire of England has furnished for them an arena
in diplomacy, in commerce, in politics, and at the bar,
which was fitted still further to excite and to display
these truly consummate powers. However justly we
may criticise or complain of the universities of England
for doing so little for science, or philosophy, or even
for the best kind of philology, we ought never to overlook what they have done for the training of the men
who have wrought the deeds, and uttered the thoughts,
and inspired the sentiments which have made England
so great. But while the universities have so efficiently
trained their honor or class-men, it is the universal testimony, that the pass-men have been as grossly neglected.
And why ? Chiefly because they are not held to the
responsibility of *daily work under the pressure of a constantly impending necessity.* We would not, if we could,

imitate their *pass system* with its irregular attendance at
lectures, its feeble and intermitted supervision, its persistent and allowed dissipations and extravagance, its
foolish waste of money and its more fearful waste of
time and opportunity. We cannot imitate their *class
system* if we would, because we have no such prizes
as they possess by which to enforce and stimulate
labor. The university of Oxford distributes yearly
in scholarships, fellowships, etc., the sum of 120,000
pounds sterling, the hope of sharing in which, excites
some four or five hundred reading men. It may be
safe to dispense with daily examinations for reading
and honor-men when the hope of such rewards constantly inspires and impels to labor. The failure of
such a system to influence the pass-men to constant industry, and often even to the appearance or profession
of such industry, should warn the American colleges
against any similar relaxation in the tension of the
feeble incitements which they can apply.

The German system has also prizes in the civil and
professional appointments, which are determined by the
result of every examination from the beginning of the
gymnasial to the end of the university life, and which
are most powerfully reinforced by the intense and prevailing intellectual activity of the cultivated classes.
But the German system fails effectively to reach the
lower two-thirds of the university men, notwithstanding all that the rigid and compulsory training of the
gymnasium has previously done for them.

As to the objection, or the sentiment on which it is
founded, that to labor under compulsion or for marks is
degrading to the manhood of the pupil ; neither seems

to us to require consideration or discussion. The constraint is moral, and is of precisely the same character which meets a man all his life long. It is only made more definite and efficient in the college. It neither excludes nor weakens the nobler motives of self-culture and of duty, the motives derived from the love of learning, or from a desire to be useful to man and to do honor to God. Marks for what a man is and does are everywhere noted for or against him, with more or less justice, as long as he lives, and for all his efforts, in the judgments of his fellows, and, as we are taught, even in the books of the Eternal Judge.

We object, then, most strenuously to the substitution of the occasional examination for the daily recitation, because wherever it has been used it has failed even under the most advantageous circumstances ; because it can be applied in the American colleges with a comparatively feeble efficiency ; and because the stimulus and training involved in constant and required intellectual application, is more needed and is less valued in this country than in any other. A few self-educated men reach the same results on similar conditions in different circumstances, as the lamented Lincoln forced himself to master Euclid's geometry, and learned in that way to master his own intellectual powers. But the great mass of our ruling minds, and among them a considerable number of college graduates, are shrewd and quick-witted, rather than reflective and self-directing— men of intense intellectual activity and exalted self-confidence, rather than patient and scrutinizing seekers after truth. What is worst of all, many of them are men of little reverence for truth and small confidence in

principles ; in part because they have never been taught
to know the value and dignity of conscientious, thorough, and methodical work. They believe in getting
on by their wits rather than by work—which often sig-
nifies by little of wisdom and less of honesty.

If there is any country where the sobering and disciplining influence of a vigorous but enlightened training
from books is needed, or where it is fitted to be most
efficient, it is in a country like this. If there is any
country where those who themselves have had experience of the benefits of college discipline, and have seen
its power over their fellows, and to whom, withal, is entrusted the direction of the discipline and instruction of
wealthy and influential seats of learning, should be slow
in relaxing the efficiency of its forces, it is the country
in which presumptuous demagogues, both lay and clerical, editorial and speech-making, cry one thing one day
and another thing the next, and where quacks in education, religion, and politics of every variety and degree
find a ready hearing and devoted partisans.

A continued residence at college, or *keeping one's terms*,
has been esteemed important in all the American colleges.   Such residence has ordinarily been required as
a condition for the first degree.   The practice of shortening the course by over-leaping a year or a term, or of
presenting one's self for examination at any time, has
not been allowed, on the general theory that no person,
unless in very extraordinary circumstances, can perform
the work of two years or of two terms in one, and therefore no one should be admitted to examination in advance of his standing.   This practice and the theory
on which it is founded, are called in question by some,

and the doctrine is advanced and occasionally put in practice, that residence and class standing should both be disregarded, provided the pupil can pass the prescribed examinations. So much prominence has of late been attached to competitive examinations all the world over, that the importance of residence and continued study has been somewhat overlooked, and it would not be surprising if the practice should be recommended and introduced in some colleges of ceasing to require continued or regular residence, and of throwing open the examinations for degrees—possibly for honors—to all well-accredited applicants.

We do not propose to argue the subject of residence at length. It will come up again in another connection. We will content ourselves by citing the following testimony of Matthew Arnold, in respect to the German practice :

" A public school-boy, who, to evade the rule requiring two years in *prima*, leaves the gymnasium from *secunda*, goes to a private school or private tutor, and offers himself for examination within two years, needs a special permission from the minister in order to be examined. So well do the Prussian authorities know how insufficient an instrument for their object—that of promoting the national culture and filling the professions with fit men,—is the bare examination test; so averse are they to cram ; so clearly do they perceive that what forms a youth, and what he should in all ways be induced to acquire, is the orderly development of his faculties under good and trained teaching.

" With this view all the instructions for examination are drawn up. It is to tempt candidates to no special

7

preparation and effort, but to such as a scholar of fair ability and proper diligence, may, at the end of his school course, come to with a quiet mind and without a a painful preparatory effort tending to relaxation and torpor as soon as the effort is over. The total cultivation *(Gesammtbildung)* of the candidate is the great matter, and this is why the two years of *prima* are prescribed, 'that the instruction in this highest class may not degenerate into a preparation for the examination, that the pupil may have the requisite time to come steadily and without over-hurrying to the fullness of the measure of his powers and his character ; that he may be securely and thoroughly formed, instead of being bewildered and oppressed by a mass of information hastily heaped together.' All *tumultuarische Vorbereitung,* and all stimulation of vanity and emulation is to be discouraged, and the examination, like the school, is to regard *das Wesentliche und Dauernde*—the substantial and enduring. *Perverse studet qui examinibus studet,* was a favorite saying of Wolf's." *(Schools and Universities,* etc.)

We had proposed to treat distinctly of the class system which is almost universally adopted in the American colleges. It has not escaped severe criticism, and at present is likely to be exposed to still more earnest objections. It must stand or fall with the retention or abandonment of the several features which we have noticed, viz., a prescribed curriculum, an enforced and daily recitation, and a continued residence or keeping of terms. Some of its more important relations, as a means of intellectual culture and excitement, will need to be considered when we come to speak of the American college as a society having a common and organic life.

These several features of the American college system involve of necessity a constant enforcement of faithful study by the instructors, and a vigorous application of stringent discipline. A curriculum, frequent recitations and constant residence, can have no force or effect unless they are prescribed and enforced as law, and are made the conditions of enjoying the advantages and reaping the rewards which the college holds in its gift. This is so obvious as to need no elucidation. Young men who are too manly in their spirit, and too independent in their feelings to acquiesce in such a discipline, are too old in their feelings to be members of a college, however young they may be in years. A year's trial of the discipline of a banking or trading house, on shipboard, or in the army, might set them back a half-score of years in fancied age, and serve to correct somewhat their ideas of the consistency of manliness with responsibility and supervision. Their confident advisers of the press who recommend the abandonment of supervision and constraint over such high-minded youths, may be properly advised in turn to try the experiment in their own printing offices and among the members of their own editorial corps.

VI.

THE EVILS OF THE COLLEGE SYSTEM AND THEIR REMEDIES.

We neither overlook nor deny the evils of the college system. The evils attending upon its administration are neither few nor slight. The spirit of routine is constantly ready to take possession of both instructors and pupils, inducing in the one the mechanical and perfunctory performance of duty, and, in the other, the constrained and enforced preparation of lessons. The pupil is constantly in danger of regarding the lesson as a task imposed, and of overlooking both the necessity that tasks should be imposed, and the fact that every task brings the opportunity for intellectual energy and improvement. Other modes of employing and improving the mind which are more exciting, or are rewarded by the acclaim of one's society or one's set, such as rhetorical exercises and feats of reading and debate, or striking acquisitions out of the common line, whether in science, or letters, or in achievements less intellectual, are constantly preferred to the more sober and common-place duties of the college work. The resort to all sorts of expedients to meet the enforced recitation, the use of assistance to avoid dishonor or discredit, excessive cramming for those examinations which, properly used, furnish the best of opportunities for a leisurely review, and the prevalent attitude of antagonism against, instead of coöperation with, the aims of instructors, are too widely prevalent and too notorious to be denied or overlooked. The disposition to find in the unconstrained pursuit of favorite studies for the fancied future an excuse for the neglect of studies that are imposed in the present, is fearfully prevalent. Self-reproach for neglect, or chagrin at disappointed expectations, or vexation at some real or fancied injustice, is made the pretext or excuse for persistent idleness and systematic neglect. The college studies are declared by consent to be a bore, even by many who derive from them no inconsiderable advantage. Even the most faithful and conscientious students are deterred from pursuing their studies in the most enlightened spirit, and from perfecting and fixing them by additional thought and research, through the influence of associations which their better judgments resist, and of a prevailing sentiment of which in their hearts they are ashamed. Studying for rank and cramming for immediate effect, both tend to dwarf the love of knowledge itself and to induce bad intellectual habits.

The instructors, also, are in danger of being either vexed or discouraged, and so of becoming unsympathizing with and distrustful of their pupils. Their best instructions are not always listened to, or are not appropriated, through the impatience or the listlessness of their constrained and wearied pupils ; often " cabined, cribbed, confined," through the poverty of the college, in low and ill-ventilated class-rooms. The perpetual inculcation of elementary knowledge becomes wearisome and disgusting to the men whose sympathies with the young are not perpetually renewed. The experience of the same failures, the same mistakes, and the same follies is wearisome to the spirit. The antagonism and slyness of his pupils tend to evoke inhumanity and suspicion in the teacher. Hence the want of earnestness and hopefulness, of courage and patience, sometimes the want of interest in the truths imparted and in the pupils to whom they are given, which occasionally settle down upon the mind and heart of the half-paid and unthanked college teacher, which paralyze his efforts, and eat out his life, and sometimes make him pedagogical, hard, and dry, or supercilious, distant, and " Donnish."

Not a few of these evils are incidental to any system of instruction, whether optional or enforced. The few that are occasioned by the enforced curriculum of the college, would, if it were abandoned, be exchanged for others more serious, and their name would not be small. It is, however, a fair and important question, by what expedients can they be obviated and the college system retained,—as it must be, or be sacrificed at the cost of evils manifold greater and more numerous ?

In answer to this question, we beg leave to offer the following suggestions :

First of all, an adequate and somewhat uniform preparation of knowledge and power should be sought for in the students, and as far as possible should be required. We would allow great liberality in the trial of candidates, but if, after trial, any are found hopelessly deficient, they should be sent down either to another class or to a thorough-going coach, who will either drive them up to their duty, or discipline them to better habits of study and acquisition. The men who are best prepared and whose previous studies in any way make it easy for them to master the college work, should, in case the class is divided into different sections, not be allowed to go into the section of lowest attainment, but should be compelled to keep up to the line which is fairly within their reach. Such men should be stimulated, if possible, by some additional work for honors or prizes, especially in extra classical reading, or in mathematical problems.

As it is notorious that not a few enter college with a superior classical preparation, and have abundant time for extra reading, they ought to be encouraged to this by a special examination in some author not read by the class, at which honors should be given to all who acquit themselves well, and success be made to count in the estimate of the college standing. This examination should require something more than the ordinary studying which is exacted in the recitation room. By a similar method, encouragement for special studies in all departments of knowledge might be systematically allowed. In order to provide for such studies and examinations, as well as to give somewhat more freedom and variety to the curriculum, it would be necessary that the time of the students should be less cut up by an excessive number of exercises.

There are many reasons, indeed, why, in the later years of college life, the recitations should not be so frequent, in order to avoid this evil of an excessive division of the time ; as also that the exercises themselves might be less exclusively exercises of recitation, and might admit more and more largely the element of instruction. It would be most desirable if the instructor of every class should seem to be a fellow-worker with his pupils as in the English Universities. At least the habits of college recitations would be greatly improved if the pupils should be allowed to express their own difficulties or misgivings, or ask questions for information and guidance. To this end the apartments should be made attractive and convenient, and liberally provided with every accessory in the way of apparatus and illustrations. No classical room would be any the less agreeable if its walls were hung with attractive maps and photographs. The instruction need be none the less severe and exacting, if the students were allowed to breathe a respirable atmosphere, or to sit on comfortable benches. The hopeful son of Tim. O'Flaherty is better accommodated at the age of ten in the palatial public school-houses that are voted him by our sovereigns, than is the delicate son of a millionaire in the class-rooms of colleges which have educated thousands of the intellectual princes of the land.

The instruction of the colleges should be made as intellectual and as wide-reaching as possible, in order that the drilling processes should justify themselves continually to the judgment of the most stupid and faithless. Even the driest analysis of word or sentence and the most rigid processes of the mathematics may be enlivened with some interesting illustrations and applications, provided the instructor be a man of intellectual breadth and have a desire to stimulate and enlarge the minds of his pupils. The teacher of the classics may teach much of English if he will, while he professes to instruct only in Greek. Geography, history, and æsthetical criticism can scarcely be with-holden if the teacher has a well-stored and generous mind. We have already expressed the opinion that a less strictly grammatical and a more liberal character should be given to classical study in the advanced years of the course.

It would not be amiss if more frequent instruction and incitements of a general character were furnished in respect to the opportunities for improvement which attend each of the stages of college life, and occasional free and friendly communications were made respecting the hindrances and aids to self-culture and the best methods of making the most of the college curriculum. Perhaps there is no point in which students err more seriously than in respect to the use of their leisure, the selection of private or special studies, the direction of their reading and the cultivation of facility in writing and in speech. In short, while the disciplinary pro-cesses should be enforced with the utmost rigor, in or-der that they may be efficient, the intellect of the pupils should be treated as little as possible as a mechanical recipient and should be stimulated and enlarged as rapidly as possible to independent and rational activity. This is possible only on the condition that the instruct-ors are men of generous intellectual training, that they are not so overworked as to become mere educational drudges, and that they give the best of their energies to the work of teaching and of training. The instruct-ors of a college should be men who are not merely at home in their own departments, but who understand and appreciate their relations to other sciences and to life. Otherwise they cannot teach in the liberal spirit

and with the generous effect which are to be desired.
They should not be overworked in the college by being
tasked too many hours to allow them to make progress
in their favorite studies and to retain their freshness
and vigor for work in the class-room. Nor should they
be overworked by extra labors out of the college to gain
the living which they fairly earn and which the college
ought to provide. They should also give the choicest
of their energies and zeal to the service of the college
as instructors.

The more widely cultured an instructor is, the more
liberal will be the spirit and effect of his teaching, all
other things being equal. Consequently to deliver the
colleges from the tendencies of routine, they must be
provided with men of liberal culture and varied intellectual endowments. The influence of such teachers
is not, however, limited to the spirit and manner of
their direct instructions. The presence of and contact
with a man of such a description, who occupies the
place and exercises the functions of an instructor, is
itself both instruction and inspiration of the most effective character. The driest exercises become fresh
when conducted by such teachers, and the most monotonous routine is varied by their admonitions and sympathy. The regular professors and instructors should
also be the chief reliance of the college for the purposes
of discipline and instruction, and even for the ends of
incitement and enthusiasm. Irregular and extraordinary
lecturers can do little to supply their deficiencies, and
also very serious injury when they seem to be most inspiring. No mistake can be more serious than that to
suppose that a college gains very largely by adding to

its corps of professors eminent personages, who have little or no active concern with the business of instruction or who come rarely in contact with the students. The continued presence of a resident professor of acknowledged eminence, or the occasional appearance of a non-resident lecturer of popular renown, neither of whom holds a constant and intimate connection with the processes of instruction and moulding that are every day forming and exciting the minds and characters of the students, is of comparatively little significance. To attach to the roll of a college a list of names of men eminent for science or learning, whose connection with its work is occasional only, may gratify the vanity of its patrons and sound largely in the ear of the American public, but it adds little of strength, and may impart much of weakness, to the efficiency of the corps. By the same rule, to found so-called chairs of instruction which shall serve as comfortable provisions for the real or professed devotees of special sciences, may promote the cause of science (in a questionable way), but it does not add to the energy or effect of the college or university as a place of training. Even science is furthered in a questionable way by such endowments, for the reason that the man who is called to the constant service of instruction, is far more likely to make advances in his own department than the man who is installed upon an endowment of which study, and not teaching, is the chief object. The German professors lecture their one or two hours a day through the academical year, and yet they do far more for science than the Fellows at Oxford who are held to no duties of instruction at all.

There should be a constant advance in the matter and power of the instruction with the advance of the students in knowledge, in intellectual tastes, and intellectual power, as well as in the self-reliance and responsibilities of manhood. The student of the Freshman year is a very different being from the student of the Senior year and he requires instruction and incitements of a different description. The one has not wholly ceased to be a boy in his intellect and his character. The other has begun to feel himself somewhat of a man in both. It is senseless to absurdity, to instruct or to govern the two by precisely the same methods. We have already given our reasons for modifying the methods of classical instruction, with the progress which the professor may presume in the student —which he has a right to assume as the ground of his instructions ; and which if he does not assume, he may dwarf and belittle the intellect and character of his pupil by the very earnestness and energy with which he persists in treating him as a school-boy. The worst thing that can be said about the college system as at present administered, is that it keeps the students too completely in leading strings by training them for a series of years too exclusively after the same exacting and mechanical methods. It should be the constant aim of the instructor to avoid and overcome this tendency by quickening the intellect and stimulating the enthusiasm of his pupils as efficiently as possible. As they advance towards manhood he should teach and treat them more and more as though they were men. He should rise above their knowledge and aspirations, rather than fall below them. He will do them no harm

if at times he presumes that they know more than they
do, provided he understands how to recur to elementary truths and principles, and how to exemplify these
in their remoter and more elevated applications.   Some
insist as we have seen, upon the gradual abandonment
of recitations and the substitution of lectures on the
ground that the instructor should teach more and ex-
amine less, as the student becomes more mature.   For
this among other reasons they advocate the gradual introduction of the university system to the higher classes
in order to exorcise the school-boy spirit.   Many younger
professors who are *fresh from* the lectures of foreign
universities show their *freshness to* the American college by judging that *to lecture* is alone synonymous with
to instruct.   They overlook the fact that the most effective instruction is that which is personal and familiar,
and also that a college pupil who is compelled to work
and to give account of his performances is far more
promising than a college school-boy who is inflated with
a belief in his capacity to take knowledge chiefly by
the ear.   Dependence and docility, even if carried to
excess, are better in the long run than cramming and
conceit.   Others have sought to deliver the college
from the evils in question by introducing a great variety of studies into its curriculum or by making many
optional.   To elevate the student to manly efforts and
manly tasks, they would give him the taste of several
liberal studies or at least the choice between several,
especially in the later years of the course.   But sad experience has proven that to crowd too many important
studies upon the attention just as the mind is awakened
to respond to their importance, is often to weary, be-

wilder, and discourage it.   To force the student to make imperfect preparation by excessive tasks, is ill fitted to excite that courage and hope which come only from actual achievement.   To give him the choice between several is often to tempt him to work excessively and superficially, or to avoid the most difficult although confessed to be the most important duties, or to follow an ignorant or factitious preference under the name of obeying a prevailing taste.   Indeed both the listlessness and unnatural cramming for marks and honors with which the colleges are now afflicted are in great part owing to the enforcement upon students, of studies too high for their capacities, too numerous for thorough mastery, or too monotonous for ordinary patience.   To attempt to avoid or prevent these evils by voluntary attendance upon lectures would be to go further in a wrong direction.   The system of lecturing allows the teacher to be almost a stranger to his pupils and his pupils to be strangers to him.   That close personal acquaintance and sympathy which is the only condition of successful instruction can be secured only by the system of recitations.   To deliver the colleges from the mechanical and school-boy routine which are so justly complained of, we need first of all a system of skillful, progressive, and varied instruction which shall keep pace with the growing capacities and the advancing tastes of students.   To devise and enforce such a system, a corps of able and devoted instructors is required who shall apply to their work the best energies of well trained and enthusiastic minds.   No selection of studies and text books, however wise and progressive, will of itself educate a body of students.   No system of discipline however skillfully devised will enforce itself. All men tire of mere routine—impatient and sensitive youth, above all—however essential its pressure and repetition may be to discipline, unless the routine be made living and adaptive by the skill and sympathy of a teacher who is a sympathizing friend and guide as well as monitor and overseer. It is, then, of the first importance that the instructors who man our colleges should be men of high general and special culture. It is equally important that such men should not merely be attached to the college, but should become its working forces by actually coming into frequent contact with the students as efficient instructors. The proposal to attach a species of university chairs to the American colleges, to be filled by eminent *savants* or *specialists* who shall simply give a few lectures with the hope of stimulating and exciting the students, is founded on a serious misconception of the actual working of the college system.

It would be far better for the efficiency of the college system if there were attached to every large college a corps of Fellows to whom should be assigned special duties of instruction in a private and familiar way, and whose intercourse with the students should diffuse a spirit of culture, and of enthusiasm for self-improvement. Such Fellows might be elected in special departments, as in Greek, Latin, English Literature, History and Mathematics ; in each of the Natural Sciences, and Philosophy. They should be elected, not advanced on examination, that college rank alone need not determine their position, but the capacity to receive and impart culture, and general desirableness for the higher considerations of character and promise. They should be elected for a term of years, that the spirit of sloth and self-indulgence should neither in fact nor in appearance be fostered by a life pension. They should be elected to an office with definite duties, as examiners, as critics of composition, as coaches to the timid or the halting, above all as private or parlor teachers to special classes who might desire improvement, and as inspiring friends to the whole community. They should be advanced to the post of private teachers in their special studies after they have themselves been admitted to the degree of Doctor of Philosophy. The provision for their support should be ample enough to satisfy one who is animated with a desire for knowledge and self-improvement, or who aspires to a literary career as instructor, editor, or *littérateur*, and liberty should be given to teach privately, for pay, only to a limited extent. The presence of such a body of studying and teaching Fellows would, it is believed, be most efficient in elevating the tone of the whole academic body. Being fresh from the undergraduates, they would retain their academic sympathies and traditions. Occupying a quasi-official position, and being entrusted with certain duties, they would feel their responsibility to use their influence in the right direction. The addition of such a corps of honorary students and teachers would do much towards elevating the college to the real efficiency and the generous spirit of the university. One hundred thousand dollars expended in the endowment at Yale or Harvard College of six or eight such fellowships, terminable in from five to eight years, would do more to furnish the country with a real university than the expenditure of a million in founding a new institution on a scale of magnificent expectations. Such a body of Fellows would also serve as a school for the training of permanent instructors.

On the same principle and for similar reasons, we deem it absolutely necessary to the best efficiency of the college system, that much of the instruction should be given by young men who are fresh from the experience of college life. This brings up the much vexed question whether Professors should in all cases be preferred to Tutors. Upon the first view it would seem that instruction by a Professor is in all cases to be preferred when it can be had, because he has a permanent interest in, as well as responsibility for the institution and the department to which he is devoted, and because study and experience will render him more competent and successful. For these reasons it has been confidently inferred that permanent instructors, whether Professors or Tutors, who have taken a department as a life work, are greatly to be preferred. On the other side it is to be said, that a man fresh from his college experience brings to his work a knowledge of the latest college generation. As a young man he is naturally more accessible to the young than an older person, is more ready to appreciate their difficulties and to sympathize with their embarrassments and their successes. Above all he is capable of greater labor and for many reasons is more patient under it, and is therefore more likely to be exacting, thorough, and persevering. In discipline also he is more resolute, more zealous, and more enterprising. A professor equally young is often not as valuable or efficient an officer as a tutor. The newly acquired official position of the professor is sometimes an embarrassment to his success. The necessity of providing so great a number of permanent officers as a large college requires, would involve the serious risk of hasty appointments which might entail upon the college the evil of an inferior or undesirable officer for a long lifetime. The introduction yearly into the academic body of one or two new members who are free from the more serious responsibilities which rest upon the Professor, is a renewal of fresh and young blood, without which the body tends to traditionalism, stagnation, or official stiffness. Moreover, the fact is not to be forgotten or overlooked that the improvement of our colleges, as their resources increase, will necessarily involve a very great increase in careful personal tuition. The classes must be subdivided into very much smaller divisions, especially in the earliest years. It follows of necessity that the greater minuteness of personal instruction, as well as the increase of personal sympathy, will involve the necessity that the tutorial as contrasted with the lecturing function should be in more abundant request. For these and other reasons we regard the tutorship as essential to the efficiency and life of any considerable college. The office ought, however, to be placed upon a better footing than it is at present in most colleges. The salaries should be very considerbly increased. The tenure should be longer, as it would be if the office were more lucrative. The office should as far as practicable be made a training place for the professorate by limiting the duties and studies of the tutor to special departments. With a few fellowships amply endowed ; an able corps of efficient tutors handsomely paid, and to whom should be accorded the honor which they justly deserve of being indispensable to the successful working of the college system ; and with a full corps of professors in the several departments of literature and science, the college would need nothing except that all these officers should be the best who are attainable.

Much would be accomplished for the unity and effective working of the college system as well as for the awakening of a generous enthusiasm for knowledge and improvement, if the heads of those departments in which are associate professors and tutors could exercise a personal supervision of the instruction that is given.   The teaching which they can give personally must be confined to a single class.   But if they could also have leisure and opportunity to inspect and direct the teaching of others, if they could, as a part of their duty, visit the class-rooms of their proper subordinates, they might do much to quicken the zeal of both teachers and pupils.   This method is practiced at West Point with the happiest results.

Many other expedients might be devised to give greater efficiency to the college system, without relaxing in the least from its thoroughness or departing from those traditions which experience has established and confirmed.

We owe some apology, perhaps, for bringing before the public these suggestions of detail in which they have little interest, and in respect to the merits of which they are scarcely competent to form an opinion. We mean no disrespect when we say that the American public, even that part of it which is made up of the graduates of colleges, are as unfitted to advise in respect to the details of the management of a college as they are to direct the details of managing a railway, a cotton mill, or a trading house. We shall therefore say no more upon the subject before us. The discussion of it thus far in these few particulars, may serve to convince our tribunal that those most familiar with these institutions are as well acquainted with their defects and as sensitively desirous that they should be removed as are the public who criticise them so freely. A few topics of more general interest remain, upon which we still ask a hearing.

VII.

THE COMMON LIFE OF THE COLLEGE.

The most of the topics which we have in mind relate to *the college as a community.* Sufficient prominence is not always given to the social and common life which characterizes most of the American colleges. There are a few of these institutions, it is true, in which these influences are not especially noticeable. Those colleges in our large cities in which nearly all the students reside at home, and none live in common lodgings, have a much less marked and energetic public life. The students in these institutions are not shut up to the society of one another. They are not separated from the life of the family ; for this continues to exert its accustomed, though a somewhat divided influence. The excitements of society out of the family are as much within the reach of the student as before he entered college, and are likely with the progress of his student-life to be more and more attractive and engrossing. .The intellectual influences of the students upon one another are mainly restricted to the class-room and the occasional debate. They do not proceed from a social life which is created by residing in common lodgings, eating at common tables, and participating in common conversations, sports, and festivities.

Those colleges in which the number of students is very small, furnish a public opinion, which, it may be, is less active for evil; possibly one that is less efficient and controlling for good. It may not be easy to analyze this subtle but most potent agency into its various elements and to assign to each constituent its relative force. Indeed the product itself is far from being a constant quantity. It is not the same in any two institutions ; each individual college having a *genius loci* of its own, which is in part dependent on traditionary influences and in part affected by the force of living men and of current events. This spirit varies in the same college, and it may be with each college generation. There are, however, a few salient features that are common to all these colleges and that are active at all times, which it is not difficult to enumerate.

These influences are not always adequately estimated even by those who have enjoyed the exhilaration and have been stimulated by the force of this highly oxygenated atmosphere. Those who have not experienced them find it difficult to estimate them at their real value, and often listen with incredulous questionings to the representations of their great importance, or look with silent wonder upon the excitement which they occasion in the young collegian as he begins to feel the stimulus of this peculiar life, and in the gray-headed student whenever he greets an old classmate with an unmistakable heartiness or reverts to the scenes of his college life with a special enthusiasm. It is important that they should not be overlooked in any attempt to vindicate the college system against the prejudices or misconceptions which are entertained by its censors and judges of the American public. Possibly the discussion may result in a higher appreciation of the indispensable value of such an agency in a state of society like our own and of the duty resting upon the philanthropist and the patriot to make it more efficient and abundant in its influences for good.

The college community is emphatically an *isolated* community ; more completely separated and farther removed than almost any other from the ordinary and almost universally pervading influences of family and social life. When the student leaves his home to enter college, it is true that in a most important sense he leaves it forever. He literally leaves father and mother, not in his affections or his respect ; for both of these feelings may remain with him and grow stronger and tenderer with absence and the progress of years ; but he does leave them in respect to the controlling power which they are to exert over his opinions, sentiments, and aims. He may do this unconsciously and most unwillingly, but he does it none the less truly and emphatically. When the father has carefully provided for the comfort of his son in the apartments which are henceforward to be his new home, he little thinks of the import of what he has done. When the mother takes her affectionate and most anxious leave of the boy who goes forth into his new life, she little dreams how true it is that she loses him as a boy forever. The public opinion of the little community which has hitherto formed his aspirations and his hopes, his principles and his prejudices, is henceforth to cease to be controlling ; in the future it will either entirely give way to another, or will share with it a disputed and divided influence.

The public opinion of that larger community of mankind which had begun to be felt through the openings which the family life had allowed, is swept away by the new atmosphere that rushes around him, and gradually but quickly becomes all-absorbing and controlling. Removed from the restraints of home, not yet subjected to the restraints and responsibilities of society and its public opinion, the college student is abruptly introduced into an isolated and peculiar community, which is eminently self-contained and self-sufficing, most energetic in its action and all-pervading in its presence. This common opinion is sensitive and changeable ; often it is capricious and unreasonable ; it exerts over all the members of the commonwealth a subtle and resistless fascination. Something of this influence is exerted in a large public school—but the influences of the college community are immensely more energetic and enduring. This is owing to many reasons. The college student is older, and though for that reason he should be less pliable and more self-relying and independent, yet the first form in which the developing man asserts his being is ordinarily to attach himself to a society of those who like himself are ready to withstand the control of his " natural enemies." It is no paradox to say that the first essay of the student's independence is often an act of prostrate subserviency to the opinion of the college community. This opinion he at first has little share in forming ; he does little else than yield himself to the sentiment which he finds already formed. This community has its traditions, which are represented to be sacred by age and uniform observance ; its customs, which are so ancient that the mem-

ory of man runneth not to the contrary, *i. e.*, for one
college generation ; its self-constituted and venerable
lawgivers in the guise of certain loud mouthed personages who are often little better than disguised sons of
Belial ; its natural aristocracy of eminent scholars, distinguished writers, prize and honor men, boating men,
and gymnasts. To these should be added its ladies'
men, its fancy men, its fast men, its witty men, and its
stupid and silly men, through all the varieties of the
Dii majorum et minorum gentium who make up the college mythology. It is eminently a law unto itself, making and enforcing such laws as no other community
would recognize or understand ; laws which are often
strangely incongruous with the usually received com-
mandments of God and man. It has standards of
character which are peculiar to itself, unlike those
which the great world recognizes, but which are well
understood and most efficient within its own limited
circle. It has an intellectual atmosphere of its own,
stimulating to extraordinary and long continued labor,
and to austere self-denial ; sometimes unwise in the aims
and methods of activity which it enforces. Its social
customs, laws, and criteria, are the products of its isolated and peculiar life, and are an unsolved mystery
to all other societies. Its ethical and religious life is
marked by singular excellences and as striking incon-
sistencies and defects ; sometimes sinking far below the
rules and attainments of men in other communities and
again soaring loftily above them. No community
is swayed more completely by the force of public opinion. In none does public opinion solidify itself into so
compact and homogeneous a force. Before its power

the settled judgments of individual conviction are often abandoned or overborne, the sacred associations of
childhood are relaxed, the plainest dictates of truth and
honor are misinterpreted or defied. Notwithstanding
the unnatural virulence of the morbid epidemics with
which this community is occasionally visited, and the
steady operation of certain endemic tendencies to evil,
justice requires us to assert that the prevailing influences are not only healthful but are eminently vitalizing. In no community of persons of immature age
is the intellect more likely to be efficiently awakened,
and on the whole to be more wisely directed, than in
this commonwealth. In none is real merit more likely
to be discerned, or when discerned is it more gener-
ously acknowledged. In no community are the factitious distinctions of life, as of wealth, birth, and manners, of so little account in comparison with intellect,
generosity, and openheartedness. In none do the rich
and poor meet together on terms more honorable to the
rich and more acceptable to the poor, than on the arena
dignified by the presence of earnest intellectual labor,
and cheered by the sunshine of youthful generosity.
In none are shallowness, pretension, and shams more
quickly discovered or treated with a more unanimous
derision. In no community in which young men live
together are that conceit and assumption which are as
natural to many youth as teething is to infancy, more
effectually rebuked and more quietly abandoned. Even
the resident traditionary follies and sins of the place,
its antagonism against the faculty and the law, the occasional frightful evasions and untruth in the acts and
words of otherwise honorable and honest students in

their dealings with the government, and the jealousies and feuds between classes and factions, are many of them exaggerated and perverted excellencies. Even the very "failings" of college students, however inexcusable and injurious they are, may be truly said to "lean to virtue's side."

In respect to the moral dangers which attend a residence in this peculiar community, very superficial and very unjust impressions prevail. Our opinion is, and we believe it will be confirmed by the most extended observation and the most accurate statistics, that there is no community in which this preëminently critical period of life can be spent with greater safety than it can in the college. If needful pains were taken to describe the dangers and enumerate the failures which befall an equal number of young men selected from families of similar conditions in life, whether at home or among strangers, whether passing their youth as farmers or mechanics, as clerks or students, it would be found that the moral results alone would be in favor of the life at a well-regulated college. Many of the dangers and evils of the college are eminently short-lived, being quickly ended by their own excess and extravagance ; many are abandoned, outgrown, or repressed by means of the very intensity and publicity which they assume. Many of them are the results of artificial crises, somewhat like those which are superinduced by a physician, for the expulsion of morbific matter. Many of them are laughed at and frowned down by the better sense and the maturer experience of the older students and the more advanced classes. It is noticed in some of our colleges—and we believe it is true of

many—that some of the lower vices and the more degrading indulgences which are incident to earlier youth,
are less prevalent among the older than among the
younger classes, as the natural result of the public and
private influences exerted by the college community,
apart from any special moral or religious improvement.

The consideration of the common life of the college
is essential to a just estimate of its importance. Without it the college can neither be understood nor appreciated. It is a true and pregnant saying, " You send
your child to the schoolmaster, but 'tis the schoolboys
who educate him." The studies, the systems and methods of teaching, the knowledge and skill of the instructors, do not constitute the whole of the educating
influences of the college. Often they do not furnish
half of those influences which are most efficient, which
are longest remembered, or which are most highly valued. It is true that without the first the second could
not be exerted, for they could not exist. The more obvious and essential elements of the college also exert
upon its common life a positive and formative influence.
They do not merely serve as the necessary nucleus
around which the crystalline material is gathered in
bright and beauteous order, but they act as living germs
which shoot vitalizing influences through the organized
body. But they are not themselves the whole of the
body, nor do they include all the forces which it has at
command. Very many even of those college graduates
who have turned to the best account all the resources
which their *alma mater* could furnish, feel themselves
quite as much indebted to the educating influences of
its community for the awakening and direction of their

energies, as to their studies or their instructors. The examples of successful effort which are constantly present, the inspiration that may be derived from the striking achievements witnessed in others, the kind words of a classmate or a college-mate, the encouragement spoken at a critical moment, the prevailing estimate of literary and artistic tastes above the vulgar aspirations after wealth and power which is inwrought into the very fibres of the soul of every genuine college alumnus, his pronounced aversion to all sorts of Philistinism—the inbreathing for years of a stimulating atmosphere that is fragrant with "sweetness" and pervaded by "light;" these,—together with the warmth of college friendships, the earnestness of college rivalries, the revelations of character, the manifestations of growth, the issues of villainy and passion in retribution and shame, the rewards of perseverance and fidelity in triumph and honor—all make the college world to the student to be full of excitement in its progress and to abound in the warmest recollections in the retrospect. The men whom the student knew so thoroughly in college become ever afterwards the representatives and types of all other men ; the incidents which there occurred are examples of all other events ; its loves and its hatreds, its triumphs and defeats are those by which he ever afterwards reads and interprets society and literature, politics and history.

The intellectual stimulus and education which are furnished by the college community are of a kind which neither circumstances nor instructors can impart. They are eminently a self-education. Most of the efforts at self-improvement which are prompted by the inde-

pendent movements of one's fellows are zealously prosecuted because they are self-enforced. They fall in
with the voluntary activities of awakening manhood
and of dawning responsibility. They train to the dignity and duty of self-culture. The studies which they
directly foster and inspire are preëminently literary and
rhetorical studies, because these studies are more dependent on individual tastes and individual culture, and
from their very nature cannot be successfully prescribed
nor enforced in the regular curriculum. Studies and
ambitions of this sort are indeed not unfrequently
irregular, desultory, and unwise. They often interfere very seriously with the thorough mastery of the
curriculum of the college. Excessive attention to them
sometimes weakens the intellectual energies, induces
bad intellectual habits, depraves the taste, and perverts
the judgment. But with all these abatements, the intellectual excitement and guidance which are indirectly
furnished from the community of fellow students are to
many a man the influences of all others which leave
the strongest impression, because it is with these that
he connects the first consciousness of awakening power,
the earliest sense of independent activity and the beginnings of a steady course of self-culture. Some book
recommended by a fellow student, some incident casu-
ally occurring in the varied course of college experience, some conversation of a wise and faithful adviser,
some achievement of a classmate or friend, is remembered as a starting or turning point in the intellectual
life.

Nor are the social influences less important in the
formation of the character and the furnishing of the

man with the beginnings of all kinds of practical knowledge. It may be said that the college world is a narrow and peculiar world, is artificial and factitious in many of its workings, is greatly unlike the larger and freer world of mankind, and is therefore incapable of serving as a preparation for the actual life for which it must so soon be exchanged. Whatever may be its disadvantages in these respects, the advantages which it brings are manifold. The intimacies are most unreserved, the opportunities for the study and interpretation of character are various and long continued. It is at this period of life that the man is, if ever, proverbially frank and transparent, open and fearless. During its progress the character rapidly undergoes many transformations, which are open to the inspection of one's fellows and are often forced upon their attention. The leisure and curiosity of this morning of life, together with the zest with which its novel experiences of research and discovery are enjoyed, all contribute to give energy and interest to this study of character.

This study of character must involve the constant exercise of ethical judgments and the training of the moral powers. That there are peculiar exposures and dangers of a practical sort from this excited and one-sided life in an isolated and self-sufficing community, cannot be denied. That not a few are misled by its special temptations, not merely nor chiefly to vices and prodigalities of a grosser sort, but to a refined and subtle insensibility to good that is more insidious and not less really evil, will be confessed by many. That the moral powers often become paralyzed in some of their functions and incapable either of right judgments

or active feelings on certain classes of ethical questions, is one of those ever recurring enigmas and
scandals that puzzle and offend the looker-on. To the
guardian and instructor of one, or many victims of
these abnormal ethical paroxysms, the question will often present itself whether he ought to be more vexed or
amused at these instances of suspended animation in
the conscience. And yet with all these biasing and
perverting influences, it is found to be true that the ob-
servations and experiences of college life are often eminently effective in educating and quickening the conscience and in awakening and directing the moral
faculty. The failures and derelictions of college life,
and even the occasional paralysis of the conscience of
which we have spoken, may serve most important uses
as warnings from similar repetitions. The moral lessons of college life are indeed sometimes learned at a
painful and bitter cost. But similar experiences are
not uncommon with youth in every situation of life.
Perhaps under no circumstances can they be made with
a more wholesome and permanent ethical effect.

The religious influences of this common life should
not be omitted. We suppose that the college is a truly
Christian institution, so far as the instructions and the
faith of its teachers are concerned. There are not a
few reasons why the public life of such an institution
should be favorable to earnest religious thought and a
positive religious faith. The life of the student is necessarily intellectual and reflective ; whatever subjects
are studied, the study of them involves intellectual effort and studious attention. During the period of college life the earnest mind often encounters those ques-

tionings which require a decided answer, and it awakes to thoughts which cannot be repressed. It is haunted by the presence of mysterious realities which cannot be dismissed. The prospect of coming manhood with the responsibilities of individual character and of independent life, at once sobers and elevates. It often happens that many nearly allied as friends and classmates, are moved to similar earnest emotions and to like searching inquiries. The common sympathies of a familiar circle thus occupied quicken the better emotions and favor the happiest results. The temptations in college to sensualism and to unbelief are manifold ; but so are the influences which favor an earnest and zealous Christian life. The number of those is not small who look back to the common life of the college as the beginning or the helper of the higher life of the Christian. Were the religious influences that proceed from the colleges of this country to be withdrawn or sensibly diminished, it would seem that the Gospel itself might almost cease to be acknowledged,—so manifold are the relations of each generation of college students to the faith and life of the whole Christian Church.

The effects of these varied intellectual, social, ethical, and religious influences are so powerful and salutary that it may well be questioned whether the education which they impart does not of itself more than repay the time and money which it costs, even to those idlers at college who derive from their residence little or nothing more than these accidental or incidental advantages. The constant companionship with the members of a community professedly devoted to intellectual pursuits and elevated by literary tastes, the constantly renewed interest in those incidents which will ever break forth from its exuberant and irrepressible life, the pressure of its necessary restraints, the countless lessons of good which cannot be unheeded even by the most thoughtless and perverse, elevate the life of the merest laggard and drone at college immeasurably above the life of the luxurious do-nothing who haunts the saloons, promenades the streets, and lounges at the concerts and theatres of a large city, or who drones away the animal, most likely the sensual, life of a rich man's son in the country.

Such idlers sometimes awake to manliness and to duty when they leave college. However heavy may be the burden which they carry through life as the result of folly and waste, they rarely fail to have stored up an abundant stock of rich experiences as well as of pleasant recollections. To many who persistently neglect the college studies, the college life is anything rather than a total loss. Even those who sink downward with no recovery, find their descent retarded by the associations of dignity and self-respect with which their previous access to culture has enriched them.

We have dwelt somewhat at length upon these features of the college as preliminary to the question, Whether it is on the whole desirable that such influences should be cherished and fostered, and how far any proposed changes in the college system would be likely seriously to impair their beneficent influence?

Is it desirable that this peculiar life of the college should be retained and fostered or should it be curtailed and crippled? We reply with an indignant defi-

ance of all sorts of low and high-lived Philistines, let
it be retained! Let it not only be retained but let it
be intensified and turned to far more effective results.
We are sure that in these answers we have with us not
only the warm hearts, but the sober convictions of all
classes of collegians. The experiences of the college
life are too valuable and its manifold recollections are
too precious to be sacrificed, to satisfy the vulgar prejudices of envious illiterates, and the prosaic theories of
Quixotic reformers. Whatever else is taken from the
college, its associations, its friendships, and its inspiring influences must all remain. The low-lived utili-
tarianism of this money-loving age may grudge the
waste of a year or two to the youth who is wanted at
the counting house or in the field. The self-seeking
rivalships of hard-faced greed may scorn its generous
impulses. The sharp-faced and venal politician may
see but little *money* in *its* elections and offices. The
cold blooded realist may laugh at its romantic dreams.
The man of wide experience may sneer at the inordi-
nate conceit and the extravagant expectations of the
great men of the college year or of the college society
as " carpet-knights ;" but it still remains true that there
is in college life, with all its ignorance and its romance,
its follies and its conceit, a well-spring of living waters,
of which these Gentiles of the outer court may never
taste, and a sanctuary into which these inhabitants of
Philistia are not worthy to be admitted. Of this living fountain and this hallowed sanctuary let all the
initiated say : they shall ever be guarded by our loyal
arms as they are hallowed in our best and most generous recollections. Though the ignorant may despise
them, we know their worth, though the vulgar and pro-

saic may scorn and dishonor them, we who have drunk of these refreshing waters and wandered in these sacred shades, can never forget, because we can never lose their life-giving and ennobling influences. To all the prosaic arguments of educational reformers and the passionate appeals of envious Philistines, we lift up the triumphant song of reply, " *Gaudeamus igitur* * * * *Pereant osores, quivis antiburschius atque irrisores.*"

We will not, however, appeal solely to the feelings of those who are already convinced, nor to the unreflecting preferences of those who judge from their personal experience. We think it is susceptible of satisfactory proof that in such a country as ours, the peculiar influences of the common life of the college are of the greatest consequence, to deliver us from that gross vulgarity of taste and superficial conceit of knowlege to which it is especially exposed. Among the conservative and elevating influences which are most efficient in the promotion of general culture there are few so important as the refining influences of the college life. It takes into its organization a band of young men, at the period of life which is most susceptible of permanent influences—at the period when they are not too old to be easily moulded, and not too young to lose the forms into which they are shaped. It isolates them from the world. It surrounds and permeates their very being with the intense and quickening atmosphere of a community of youths slightly older than themselves, who are already at home in the place, and therefore masters of the situation, by means of a public opinion as overpowering as heat and as searching as light. These strangers are by natural attractions and repulsions drawn closely to one another as allies and friends, and before they are aware they begin to understand the sacred import of the words "class" and "classmate." Within the class, like soon finds its like, and friendships are speedily formed on the basis of mutual sympathy which are so closely cemented under the varied experiences of the college as to continue unbroken for life. The pursuits of this community are professedly intellectual. The thoughts and opinions of each of its members are occupied more or less predominantly with intellectual themes. The labors and anxieties, the strifes and victories, the discussions of persons and things, the loves and the hostilities, turn chiefly upon subjects of an elevated character. For four consecutive years, beginning as boys and ending as men, the members of this community make a common experience, with interruptions frequent and long enough to give greater zest to their peculiar excitements. This life has conventionalities and factitious distinctions of its own, but they are grounded on no such false and superfiicial reasons as are those of the great world without. They are far more just, more honest, more sagacious, and more generous than the distinctions of that coarser world. True manhood in intellect and character is in no community so sagaciously discerned and so honestly honored as in this community. Pretension and shams are in none more speedily and cordially detected and exposed. Whether displayed in manners or in intellectual efforts, conceit is rebuked and effectually repressed. Modest merit and refined tastes are appreciated, first by the select few and then by the less discerning many. Each individual spectator of the goings on of this active life is learning intellectual and moral lessons which he cannot forget if he would, and which he would not if he could, and he comes away with a rich freight of the most salutary experiences of culture in his tastes, his estimates of character, his judgments of life, as well as of positive achievements in literary taste and power.

Let any reflecting man think for a moment of the kind of education which society furnishes to a great extent in this country, apart from these higher influences. Let him reflect on the trickery of business, the jobbing of politicians, the slang of newspapers, the vulgarity of fashion, the sensationalism of popular books, the shallowness and cant that dishonor the pulpit and defile worship, and he may reasonably rejoice that there is one community which for a considerable period takes into its keeping many of the most susceptible and most promising of our youth, to impart to them better tastes, higher aims, and, above all, to teach them to despise all sorts of intellectual and moral shams. Whatever overweening importance the college student may attach to his own artificial life, with its factitious distinctions and its one-sided tastes, it is at least satisfactory to known that what he values and rejoices in is not in the direction of the ignoble, the selfish, the pretentious, and the trickish ; that he has been taught to honor what is true, solid, and permanent, and perhaps brings away from the scene of his discipline refined tastes for the beautiful in literature and art, which shall adorn his own life and brighten that of others. Were we to tear out of our American life the civilizing and culturing influences which proceed from college residence and college associations, we should do much to vulgarize and degrade it. If we vulgarize and degrade the life that is so depressed by materialistic tendencies, and beset by grosser temptations, we shall certainly demoralize it. We cannot safely dispense with a single agency which tends to elevate and refine this life, least of all with an agency which has been so conspicuous in its history, and been so closely interwoven with all the subtle forces of its better manifestations. It is enough for us to be able to assert that thousands of the noblest men who stand foremost in the ranks of social and professional life, would be forward to acknowledge that they are indebted to the cultivating influences of college friendships and college associations, for the germs of their best principles, their noblest aspirations and their most refined tastes.

With the views which we have expressed there are many who do not sympathize. Not a few regard the peculiar influences of college life as anything but refining, as tending rather to barbarism than to civilization, to grossness and conceit rather than to refinement and modest self-estimation. To such we have no further arguments to offer. Whether they are honestly or dishonestly ignorant and unjust, they are hopelessly irreclaimable. With those who do nothing but rail, it is useless to try to reason. There are others who propose changes which would materially modify the whole operation of the common life of the college. They would remove or introduce features which would weaken or set aside the influences which we have enumerated. They would do so with the express design of avoiding some of its alleged social evils, or with the desire indirectly to accomplish other important ends.

VIII.

THE DORMITORY SYSTEM.

The first of these changes which we notice is the abandonment of the *dormitory system.* This has been seriously urged by not a few of the friends of higher education as a most desirable improvement in the college economy. The reasons adduced in its favor are, that if the students should live in lodgings they would be brought within the amenities and restraints of the family, and be prevented from contracting the exclusive and perverse *esprit de corps*, which is thought to be the curse of colleges—that they would live, and feel and think, and act more as other human beings do, and less like that particular variety of the human species which is cloistered within the walls of a college and secluded from the ordinary influences of human society. The expensiveness to the college of providing and keeping in repair a large number of dormitory buildings is also insisted on, as well as the duty and desirableness of appropriating the money required for these purposes to objects that are more properly educational. It is often asked, "why invest so much money in brick and mortar, *i. e.*, in houses for students to dwell in, when so much is needed for salaries, for endowments, for prizes, for books, and apparatus ? It is time that the system of cloisters and quadrangles, inherited from other times,

should be abandoned with the changes required by
modern life.   More than half of the barbarism and absurdity of college life would cease if the students were
distributed generally throughout the community and in
a certain sense were members of its families, subject to
their restraints and elevated by their refining influence."

To these questions and arguments the following considerations are pertinent.   First of all, the advantages
which it is thought would follow from the distribution
of students in families cannot be realized.   It is not
easy to find, even in a very large community, a sufficient
number of families which would at once be competent
and willing to exert a wholesome influence over the
students even of a small college.   Families which are
independent in respect to income are not willing to receive lodgers, least of all students, unless they assert some claim of acquaintance or friendship.   If the
families are dependent upon the students for a part or
the whole of their living, the students will control so
many, either by a direct or indirect influence, that they
cannot be relied upon for restraint, except against the
grossest excesses, and not always against them.   The
experiment has been tried sufficiently often to be hardened into an intractable fact, that students who reside
in the most faithful and conscientious families often
succeed in making them their allies rather than their
guardians and guides, and that when a crisis or conflict
arises between the students and the faculty, the families
in which any considerable portion of them reside, even
the best and most reasonable families, more usually
side with the students than with the faculty.   If the
offense or custom of the students is not very serious in

its immediate consequences, the interference of the
faculty is complained of as officious and unreasonable.
Even if it is plainly mischievous to the community and
dangerous to life and limb, if it has often been forbidden and punished and is yet pertinaciously persisted in,
the necessary discipline of the college is often greatly
weakened by an antagonistic or at least an unsympathizing feeling in the families in which many students
reside.   It has almost passed into a proverb, that when
a college is situated in a village even of considerable
size, the college controls the public sentiment of the
community, and the faculty are compelled to contend
against the public opinion of both village and college
united.   It is often the case in a much larger community that the families in which a few students reside, or
with whom they visit, are strongly moved by their representations and their prejudices to a not inconsiderable excitement in a direction which is anything but favorable to the order of the college or the welfare of the
students themselves.   The restraints and refinements
of family life should not be expected, for they cannot
be realized in a large community of students, except
by those collegians who reside at their own homes in a
large city.   It may be questioned in respect to these
students, and in respect to all who can reside at their
homes when the college is situated in their own city
or village, whether they do not lose more by the
absence of the salutary excitements and educating restraints of the common life of the college, than they
gain by the restraints and refinements of their own families.   This leads us to observe that the residence in
dormitories by a very considerable part of the students

is absolutely essential to any vigorous and definite common life. This is foremost among the advantages of
the dormitory system. If the maintenance of such a
common life is desirable, then dormitories are essential.
The students, in order to enter into a common fellow-
ship, must have ready access to each other's society on
an equal footing. They must occupy the same prem-
ises by day and night, so that they can see one another
under every variety of circumstances. They must chat
and talk with one another as they walk and as they
lounge. They must be able to discuss the topics of
graver and of lighter interest, the politics of the country and the politics of the college ; the character of the
leading statesmen of the time, and the character of the
leading men of their class and college ; the literature of
ancient and modern times and the prominent writers of
their own circle ; the last lesson, the last lecture, the
last boat race, and the last party ; they must be able to
report and circulate the latest joke, the latest news, and
the latest *canard*. If college students are distributed
in lodgings throughout the village or city they will form
sets and associate in cliques, which, the more intimate
and exclusive they are, are likely to become more narrowing, but they cannot partake of a general public
life with its manifold cross and counter currents, its
checks and counter checks, the influence of which upon
the plastic minds of active minded and sagacious youth
is liberalizing in an eminent degree.

The dormitory system gratifies the student's desire
of independence. It fosters that feeling of self-reliance
which is suitable for his time of life, which cannot and
ought not to be repressed. At the same time it tempers

and tones it down by the manifold restraints of the community in which he dwells. At the age when a boy enters college it is usually time for him to be released from the petty and minute oversight of the domestic household and to be thrown somewhat upon himself. " The wise instructor," says Emerson, " will press this point of securing to the young soul, in the disposition of time and the arrangements of living, periods and habits of solitude. The high advantage of university life is often the mere mechanical one, we may call it, of a separate chamber and fire, which parents will allow the boy, without hesitation, at Cambridge, but do not think needful at home."

At this period of life he must in some form or other make the experiment, which is inevitable for all, of passing from the restraints of the family among those of the great community of men. He makes it under peculiar advantages, to which are incident special but not undesirable perils. He cannot be effectually nor can he be advantageously subjected to the restraints of another family than his own. It is not desirable that he should be restricted to the uncertain chances and the narrowing influences of a private and exclusive clique. It is far better, and far more safe that he should be cast upon the common life of a college which is properly restrained by skillful discipline, which is guarded by wise supervision and invigorated by a healthful ethical and religious life.

Residence in dormitories is also *morally safer* than the distribution of students in lodgings. Should it be conceded that it is attended by certain peculiar temptations, it is also attended with certain more than counterbalancing advantages, so far as it subjects the student to a more direct and ready supervision and brings him within the reach of healthful public sentiment. Residence in lodgings withdraws the student from supervision and opens abundant opportunities for secret mischief and gross vice. In those colleges in which the students are largely distributed in lodgings it is notorious that the grossest outrages against decency are plotted and executed in apartments which are remote from the inspection and interference of the college officers, and that the most deplorable examples of abandoned sensualism and sin are more frequent among those who hide themselves in remote and obscure habitations that they may indulge themselves in secret or undetected vice. Whatever may be said and said with truth of the energy of temptation and the facilities to sin which inevitably arise in a congregated mass of excitable and passionate youths, is offset by what may be said with equal truth of the restraining and elevating influences which such a community develops within itself when its sentiment is properly directed and reinforced. Residence in a dormitory is less expensive than residence in lodgings, and is therefore, in a large institution, absolutely necessary, unless such an institution is content to be a college for the rich ; which would involve a great calamity for both rich and poor. It is said that the college is not obliged to furnish lodging at a rate below that which the ordinary and natural demand would justify. We reply by two considerations. First, the college can furnish apartments in public dormitories at a cheaper rate than private parties will do it, even without loss to itself ; and second, the college may as properly furnish room rent as tuition to its pupils at less than remunerative rates to itself. But it is notorious that the instruction is furnished at less than half its cost, to both the rich and the poor. The American colleges in their theory and administration are all beneficiary institutions. As long as they remain such, it follows that public lodgings should be furnished either at comparatively high rates, because the colleges can do it more advantageously to the students, or at rates which are lower because they are beneficiary.

Public dormitories may and should be made more convenient and comfortable than private apartments. They may and should be provided with all the appliances of modern civilization, with water, gas, and heat, and every other comfort which conduces to health or morality, to neatness or self-respect. We have nothing to offer in excuse or defense for those dormitories which are not so constructed and provided, except the excuse or defense of poverty, and for this the guardians and officers are not responsible as long as they themselves suffer in common with the students. But perhaps we have delayed too long upon this topic, and therefore proceed to another. We were led to speak of the dormitory in connection with the common life of the college.

IX.

THE CLASS SYSTEM.

To this general topic we again return and observe that the *class system* is essential to an efficient and energetic common college life. The class is the organic centre, or rather one of the organic centres, the combination of which constitutes the college into an organic whole. Indeed, we do not see how an American college without fixed classes can have an efficient common life. The English universities find in the separate colleges the proper central forces, which work together into what there is of university feeling and university life. The separate colleges are distinct communities in separate buildings. The number of undergraduates in each is so small, and they are brought so frequently and so closely together, that though they may differ in age and in acquisitions, they make up a separate family, with family interests, family traditions, and family pride. Closeness and frequency of intercourse, and a sense of family honor, with their common relation to the elder fellows who eat at the same table and lodge under the same roof, unite them all by many ties and connect together men of different years and attainments by warm and intimate friendships. In the American college, the class is the charmed circle within which the individual student contracts the most of his friendships, and finds his fondest and most cherished associations. The sentiment of his class is that which influences him most efficiently, and is to him often the only atmosphere of his social life. He enters the college community as a timid and often an uncultivated novice. He meets with a company of strangers to one another and strangers to the place, its customs, and its inhabitants. These are all supposed to have reached the same grade of intellectual culture and are destined to be associates and competitors for four years in the same studies and the same amusements—in the same relations and the same rivalships. The members of this community are at once united by a sense of their common strangeness to the place and by the mutual sympathy which it engenders. This union is usually cemented by the antagonism in which this newly formed society finds itself with respect to the superior classes, and is more firmly fixed by the necessity of protection and defense. Its members soon become interested students of each other's powers and observers of each other's progress. They meet in the same class-room, or hear from one another of the achievements and characteristics of a few prominent individuals. Not a few of those who at first stand in the foreground become less conspicuous as others take their place, till under the searching tests of the class-room the capacity of each man is satisfactorily ascertained, and under the still more sagacious and nearer scrutiny of youthful companions, the character and temper as well as the practical sense and judgment of each are thoroughly tested. Like is attached to its like and the foundations of friendships begin to be laid, some of which do not survive the fortunes of the college generation, while others endure through all the changes of the earthly life. Each term has experiences and a history which is limited to the class, but in which every member of the class takes a lively interest. Each college year carries this community through its appointed cycle. As the youthful excitements of the beginning are gradually sobered into the more thoughtful anticipations that gather around the close, the fervor of its friendships increase rather than abate, till at the hour of parting the class feeling becomes more intense and the ties of its union are welded into links of iron.

But while the class is the most important society to the college student, the class itself shares largely in the sentiment of the college community, being largely formed by it and reacting upon it. The new class lives upon the common life of the whole body, while it in turn ministers to and modifies that life. It is, however, as essential to an efficient common life, as an energetic and efficient local community, whether it be township, county, or state, is essential to an energetic national life. Should the class be destroyed or set aside by the substitution of the *régime* of the university for the *régime* of the college, the energy and interest of the common life that at present characterizes the American college, must inevitably go with it. Such intimacies can only be developed by the common studies and common interests, the common enjoyments and common antagonisms of a succession of years, during the most plastic age. If we substitute for them such classes as are held together for a few weeks or months by common attendance in the same lecture-room, and allow these classes to be broken up and re-formed of new materials in new combinations, we shall lose much of the charm and more of the educating power of the college life. Whatever this common life is worth in its manifold training of the intellect to practical judgments and of the heart to its finer affections, must be sacrificed if the class system is greatly weakened or practically abandoned. The value of these influences is in our view another weighty argument in favor of retaining fixed classes, in addition to those which have already been urged.

We ought not in this connection to omit entirely another prominent feature of the college as a community, viz., the arrangements for culture and enjoyment furnished by the so-called *college societies*, secret and open, larger and smaller. These societies are common to all the universities and colleges of Europe and America. Their existence in some form is a necessary outgrowth of human nature. In similar circumstances ardent and ambitious young men will devise some expedient for self-improvement, particularly in rhetorical and literary exercises. The university cannot furnish all the culture of this sort which is required, nor if it could would it be either as acceptable or as efficient as that which is originated and managed by young men themselves. It is not surprising that in the American colleges, animated as they must be with the practical and independent spirit of the country and sympathizing most warmly with every public movement, whether political or literary, these associations should have assumed great prominence and should have exercised a powerful educating influence. The social tendencies of young men must necessarily lead to associations for other than exclusively literary purposes. The clannish tendencies which result from their ardent likings and their violent antagonisms, as well as their newly developed feelings of independence would tend to make these societies exclusive and secret. We do not propose to discuss the general question of the desirableness or the undesirableness of some associations of this sort. It is scarcely open for discussion. They are so natural to young men, indeed to men of all ages, as not to need defense or justification. Whether it is desirable that they should be secret or guarded by a mysterious reserve, and so invested with a factitious importance, admits of more question. The love of secrecy and reserve is too strong in human nature, and especially in boyish nature, to be easily thwarted. We doubt the expediency because we disbelieve in the possibility of destroying or preventing secret societies. That such societies may be, and sometimes are, attended with very great evils, is confessed by the great majority of college graduates. Prominent among these evils is the fostering of an intriguing and political spirit, which is incongruous with the general tendencies of college life toward justice and generosity ; and the division of the community and the classes into hostile factions. Whatever excesses attend them, of late hours, late suppers, noisy demonstrations, and convivial indulgencies, should be repressed by the good sense and manlier spirit of the college community. Could the continuity of many of these societies, from one college year to another, be broken up, the college life would be greatly ennobled.

The consideration of this subject suggests another
which is nearly akin, and that is whether the arrangements for social life in the college are sufficiently numerous and complete. Is it practicable and desirable
that such arrangements should be more attractive?
Some colleges have provided bowling alleys for exercise
and relaxation. Ought billiard rooms and club rooms
to be added? Is it desirable that public parlors should
be furnished, or places convenient for rendezvous and
conversation? Questions of this sort are more easily
asked than answered. It is safe to say that whatever
withdraws the students from resorts for eating and
drinking or gaming—which may furnish facilities for
other excesses—is so much gained to academic manners
and morals. An accessible and cheerful reading room,
amply furnished with the best newspapers and journals,
should be esteemed a necessity, and if it were made attractive and tasteful in its appointments and supplied
with retiring rooms for conversation, and could also be
rigidly controlled by the rules of gentlemanly etiquette,
would be a most desirable and useful agency in the
college community. The tendencies to barbarism and
roughness are manifold in the college. Jeremy Taylor
enumerates as among the miseries of our human life,
that the boy at a certain age yields himself in subjection to "a caitiff spirit." That *a caitiff spirit* prowls
around the buildings of every college and sometimes
takes possession of scores and hundreds of its inhabitants is too notorious to need any evidence. Whatever
may impede its influence or repress its manifestations
is obviously most salutary. That this spirit has sometimes been exasperated and rendered more brutal and

barbarous by barbarous methods of punishment may be safely admitted, without abating at all from the authority of any existing government or without conceding in the least to the amiable delusion that a college community can be managed without rigid authority ; and even in entire consistency with the doctrine that the government must be absolute in its commands and summary in its administration. Whatever removes the occasion for the exercise of mere authority, or even for the semblance of its assertion is, however, usually acknowledged to be a real blessing with both men and brutes, and a college student may surely take rank somewhere between the extremes of the series.

X.

LAWS AND SUPERVISION,

That a college community requires rules, and that rules must be enforced by discipline will not be disputed. That a certain measure of inspection and supervision should also be exercised over this community, to preserve decorum in the apartments and grounds, would scarcely be denied. It is not, however, easy to answer the question how minute the supervision by the college authorities should be. Upon this subject opinions differ very widely, and these opinions differ in the case of the same persons with their varying circumstances. One class of critics contend for the constant and minute supervision of a Jesuit seminary, every rule and provision of which is founded on suspicion and distrust. Another class would abandon all special rules and inspection and leave the students entirely to their own sense of honor and decorum. One class of advisers would proceed on the principle that all students are liars and scoundrels, another that they are all gentlemen and men of truth ; neither of which opinions happens to be just. The complaint is often heard and urged with special earnestness for or against this or that college, that in the one the instructors are on intimate and familiar terms with their pupils and exert over them a parental supervision, while in the other they are distant and leave the pupils to themselves. Some insist that if students reside together they should be inspected in their apartment by day and carefully locked in at an early hour by night. Others would leave them alone by day and night, without even the presence of an officer in the building in which they congregate, and to and from which they have ready access and egress at all hours. Many insist that all special laws and penalties provoke disorder and mischief, while others insist that college laws should be numerous and be strictly enforced. We cannot discuss these questions in detail, nor need we in order to vindicate the system of college residence and general supervision. The English system of locking in at an early hour is manifestly unsuited to the general freedom of our institutions, and is chiefly valuable as a security against a single vice. It is better adapted to their system of small colleges in each of which the inmates live in some sort a family life. It is the supplement or counterpoise to the greater freedom of their students in many other respects, as in daily attendance at lectures and in daily examinations of the work performed. It is in fact the single controlling influence which the college can constantly enforce, in place of which the American college has manifold more efficient substitutes. Frequent visitation of the students by day and evening has been recommended by many as essential to the faithful supervision and the parental care which the college is bound to exercise. This was practised in many of our colleges in other times and has not been entirely disused. In some instances the lodgings of students have been attached to and been alter-

nate with the residences of professors for the purpose
of making this inspection more constant and complete.
It has been generally found that such minute and constant supervision is exceedingly ungrateful and annoy-
ing, because it presents the aspect of meddling ; and it
provokes in return an antagonistic attitude in manifold
petty annoyances. The agression of constant interference provokes the resistance of boyish mischief and
arouses the wrath of the manhood that is half developed and is therefore intensely jealous for its invaded
rights. The proper medium between the too little and
the too much, is for the government to maintain and
occasionally to assert its right of visitation, and provide
for the presence in every dormitory by day and night
of officers clothed with complete authority, but to exercise its supervision chiefly by methods that are indirect.
The judgment of what students are doing and the control of their movements can be most efficiently exercised by their attendance at all the required exercises,
by constant responsibility for the work of every day, and
by the manly and scholarly sentiment of the college
community. The monitor's returns and the instructors'
record book, when closely watched and efficiently used,
if conjoined with occasional personal interviews with
students who are any way derelict are, we are per-
suaded, the most efficient as well as the least oppres-
sive instruments of official supervision. That the sentiment of the college community is far more important
and far more efficient than is commonly supposed we
have already sought to establish. It is a most interesting and important inquiry whether any system of measures can be devised by which this public sentiment can

be elevated to a higher tone and can be maintained in greater efficiency. Can any formal arrangement be made by officers, discipline, or studies which shall introduce into the community better and more elevating influences? It is manifest that such influences must to a great extent be personal and individual. The selection of officers of high personal character and of ardent and self-sacrificing devotion to the interests of the students is the first condition of success in this respect. The maintenance of a certain degree of free and familiar intercourse between them and their pupils is equally essential. The traditions of some of the colleges in this country are unfavorable to a too familiar intimacy, and the feelings of the students themselves demand a measure of reserve and isolation on both sides. Too much advice, especially if it is obtrusively administered, is if possible more offensive than too much supervision. The students themselves naturally withdraw from the society of those who are older than themselves and who hold official relations that involve some constraint on both sides. The opinions and sympathies of their fellows are of far greater concern to them than the judgments and feelings of their instructors. While all this is true there is room even under the present arrangements, for the exertion of a very efficient influence over the college community, by those who are disposed to use it. The English universities have one advantage however which we should seek to engraft upon our system. The intercourse of the tutor with his pupil is constant and intimate. It is often generous and confiding. The tutor works with his pupil and teaches him how to work. He sympathizes with his difficulties as well as corrects his mistakes. He inspires his ambitions and elevates his aims ; he liberalizes his drudgeries and imparts to the flagging somewhat of his own enthusiasm. He lays the foundation for life-long friendships, and in this way perpetuates his own influence, and the spirit of his own attainments and culture. Can we do anything of the sort? We could if we had the means. We could avail ourselves of all the advantages of the system of "fellows" and "private tutors" without many of its incidental evils. The advantages to our system of instruction of *terminable fellowships* or scholarships of the house have already been insisted on. The services which they might render as connecting links between officers and students are if possible still more important. The presence in a college community of a sufficient number of recent graduates, of eminent attainments and of attractive characters, who should share in the sympathies and have access to the opinions of the undergraduates, whose associations should be constant with the better men of all the classes, while their services as tutors and guides to the weaker should open to them abundant opportunites for befriending them intellectually and morally, could not fail to be most efficient in elevating the tone of college opinion and of college scholarship, manners, and morals. Such a provision would go farther than any other towards redeeming these communities from much of the reproach which rests upon them, however undeserved and exaggerated it often may be.

Dr. Arnold remarks more than once in his letters to this effect : if the sixth form is with me I can defy evil influences from every other source. This thought occurs

to us in connection with the inquiry whether the higher
classes,—rather, whether the highest of all, should not
have the privileges proper to a more positive manhood
than are allowed in respect to its methods of study,
relations to the instructors, and its responsibility for
the controlling sentiment of the institution.   Under the
operation of natural laws a somewhat different position
has been accorded to it in all these respects than has
been conceded to the other classes.   The studies pursued are at once more directly liberal as well as more
practical.   They are at least more practical in the
sense of having a more vital relation to the principles
which underlie individual faith and character, to the
historical and political questions which agitate the
world of living men as well as to the literature in
which men of culture find at once their refreshment
and inspiration.   The methods of instruction may be
less constrained, and the intercourse with instructors
more free and confiding.   Some have advised that the
freedom of the university should be introduced in the
closing year, and that for the selection of their studies
as well as for their responsibility in pursuing them the
Seniors should be more largely left to themselves.   We
have already given the reasons why elective studies cannot to a very great extent be allowed and why *private
studies* are to be preferred.   It is however altogether
essential to the perfection and the full development of
the college system, that the last year of college life
should be turned to its best account in self-culture.
With its beginning there begins to be developed even
to the frivolous and the idle the sense of individual responsibility for the future.   Many of the studies invite

to manly and moral reflection.   Many of them exercise
the inventive and æsthetic powers to an unwonted
degree.   All of them introduce the students to the
thoughts and opinions of cultivated men upon subjects
of comprehensive and general interest.   During this
year the student begins, perhaps for the first time in
his life, to read, and is earnest to learn how to read.
All these influences tend to awaken whatever of manhood may hitherto have lain dormant, and to quicken
into life some sense of his responsibility for his influence over the community in which he lives.   Whatever
can be done to turn these advantages to the most efficient use will elevate the tone of feeling in the whole
college.   We do not advise the release of the Senior
from any of the obligations of an enforced system of
study.   He needs them as much as ever and can profit
by them more than ever.   But he can certainly be made
to understand the value of a manly sympathy with the
decorum and order of the college and the importance
of his own influence in this regard.   It is not desirable
that he should be instructed without constant responsibility for his work.   But he may certainly be treated as
a man who has ceased to be a school boy.   The Senior
year ought to be the busiest year of all, but it ought
not to be overburdened with manifold and novel studies.
Nothing is more injurious and discouraging than the
practice of crowding a great number of liberal scientific
studies into the last year of the course, which has been
allowed in so many colleges, by way of "finishing,"
as if the student were to cease to study and learn
as soon he completes his college course.   The habits
of thorough work and the satisfaction of successful

achievement, which come from a very few things well and carefully done, are worth quite as much to the character as they are to the intellect. Whatever gives tone to either in the management of the Senior class in any American college will give elevation and tone to the sentiment of the whole community. It is not too much to labor and hope for, that in the future development of the college system the Senior class may feel its responsibility and exercise its influence for good with greater efficiency, and as a consequence the American colleges may attain a nobler and more healthful common life.

Our discussion of this common life requires us to consider the moral and religious influences which may properly be employed in invigorating and controlling it. To this subject we proceed.

XI.

THE RELIGIOUS CHARACTER OF COLLEGES.

The consideration of the American colleges as communities has brought us to the question of their religious character.   This includes several subordinate questions, such as, whether they ought to be placed under a positive religious influence, and to what extent and in what manner this influence may properly be exercised.   These questions, and many others which arise under this comprehensive topic, are from the nature of the subject not easily answered, and in the present state of opinion are involved in somewhat serious complications.

We may as well say, at the outset, that the view which any man, otherwise well-informed, will take of this subject, must necessarily vary with the views which he takes of religion itself, as to its essential nature and authority, its evidence, and its relation to man's responsibility and destiny.   It will vary also with the views which he takes of Christianity; according as he regards it as supernaturally given and historically true, or as he 'believes it to be of human origination, and, therefore, so far as its miracles and the claims and conceptions of its central personages are concerned, as more or less historically erroneous.   It will vary also according as his views are more or less enlarged of its relations to human culture, and of its friendliness to the highest forms of human development.

The position which we occupy is that " the Christian faith is the perfection of human reason ;" that supernatural and historical Christianity is the only Christianity which is worth defending or which is capable of being defended on the grounds of reason or history ; and that such a Christianity, when interpreted by enlightened judgment, as to its truths and its precepts, is not only friendly to the highest forms of culture, but is an essential condition of the same.

There are not a few at the present time who do not agree with us in this position. More than a few, we fear, of those interested in the higher education of the country, so far hesitate to receive any positive form of religion as to assume in all their reasonings, that the claims of supernatural Christianity are more likely than otherwise to be set aside in the progress of historical and scientific investigation, and that it is therefore inconsistent as well as impolitic for the universities and colleges of the country to be very positively committed to the support of these claims. Such a recognition of Christianity, in their view, hinders the freedom of investigation and of teaching, and is inconsistent with that tolerance among scholars which is required by the spirit of the age. They might repel the charge of being anti-religious or atheistic or even anti-Christian in their own faith, but they reason that for a college to recognize the Christian faith in its teachings is to commit itself to an implied bondage of opinion, which cannot but constrain the freedom of its spirit, or which must, at least, make it unwisely intolerant. We cannot accept this position or the inferences to which it leads.

We must discuss this question in an important sense from a Christian position, and judge of the whole subject from a Christian point of view. But while we frankly avow our position, we trust that it will not make us so one sided in our construction of those whose position differs from our own as to render us incapable of appreciating their difficulties or of looking at college and university education from their point of view. Though our position is distinctively and avowedly Christian, we do not propose to argue simply as theologians, or to use our assumption of the truth of Christianity as a vantage ground; but to argue as friends of education, and to occupy, so far as we may, the ground which is common to all friends of culture who are not illiberally or fanatically irreligious and atheistic in their scientific and practical theories.

The view which we shall endeavor to maintain is that the American Colleges should have a positively religious and Christian character. We have in mind the college such as we have conceived and described it,— the college which is a distinct community and maintains a separate and distinctive intellectual and social life. The few colleges which are not distinct as communities —the colleges of the very large cities, where pupils live in their own homes and are rooted in their own families —can derive their religious influence from the same sources from which other youths derive theirs, that is, from the domestic, social, and church relations of the great community from which they have never been transplanted. While it is desirable, and in a sense, necessary that institutions of this kind should exert a positive religious and Christian influence, the necessity in this case is not so imperative. We are concerned with those colleges which maintain the distinctive and intensely active common life which we have described.

When we say that the college of this description should be positive in its religious and Christian influence, we mean that the essential facts and truths of the Christian system should be recognized in all its teachings as true ; that as a community the college should participate in Christian worship, and that its instruction and discipline should, with rare exceptions, be in the hands of men of a positive and earnest Christian character.

Our reasons are the following :

First.—The colleges as such have the same duty and need of social religion which exist in every community. This can be doubted or denied only by those who deny altogether the obligation of united and common religious teaching and worship. We have seen that the college, as a community, is eminently independent and self-sufficing, deriving the roots of its life eminently from within itself, and living that life with an energy that is especially intense. If other human societies need to be socially religious, the need of the college is preëminent. If it is becoming that the great community of men should divide itself into separate societies in order that it may maintain religious teaching and worship, then it is especially appropriate that a society which is separated from every other so emphatically as is the college, should be provided with such teaching and worship. If every household ought to be a religious commonwealth, then the college which takes the youth from his home and introduces him into a larger household of its own, ought to sustain that religious teaching and worship which are appropriate to its own necessities and position.

Second.—The college, as compared with other communities, stands in special and imperative need of religious restraints and religious influences. The individuals of which it is composed have been released, sometimes abruptly, from the restraints of the family and of the public opinion of society at large. They form to themselves a public sentiment of their own, which, though often generous and just, is yet liable to strange caprices and sudden revolutions, even when sobered and elevated by the most active and ennobling religious elements. The passions are strong, the will is impetuous and weak, the judgment is immature, the experience of temptation is limited, the habits of good are not fixed, while those to evil are sometimes fearfully strong. Such a community, as it would seem, does of all others stand in pressing need of the best religious influences, and these should be constantly applied, wisely varied, and patiently maintained. If Christianity can do anything to control and elevate any class of persons, or if it is needed for any, it is adapted to and required for the susceptible, intelligent, and impetuous youth, who resort to the American Colleges.

What is adapted to the welfare of young men as in-individuals, is equally required for the order and discipline of the whole body. To govern a college by mere law, or by the force of rules and penalties, without appealing to the ethical and religious feelings of the pupils, is not always successful in the lowest sense, and it never can be in the highest. The reason and conscience must often be appealed to, and if this is done with effect, both reason and conscience must be reinforced and quickened by religious faith and feeling. If religious restraints and religious hopes are required in every community of full grown men—not as is sometimes charged to do the work of a police, but to make the work of a police less necessary,—this must be eminently true in a community of youths whose sense of propriety is not always proportioned to their knowl-edge, and whose mobile and impetuous tempers are often exasperated to resistance by rules and *surveillance.* If the college contains none whose principles of duty are made sturdy by religious reverence and whose consciences are quickened by the presence and love of God, then, on those occasions of strain and conflict between the students and the faculty which must inevitably occur from time to time, the cause of order must be imperiled. It is not according to the wisdom of experience to affirm that such exigencies will not arise, nor if they do occur, to rely upon any principles which are not enforced, either directly or indirectly, by religious faith.

Third.—It is a legitimate and important function of the college, to form the character to moral and religious excellence. Education should not and cannot be limited to the culture of the intellect and the tastes. It also properly includes the training of the character The Christian believer holds that the character can only be rightly formed when it is subjected to the authority of Christ. He holds that discipleship to Christ is the condition of complete success in the culture and regulation of the springs of action. When then he requires that the college should teach and influence its pupils according to this theory, he is only consistent with his own most sacred convictions. Whenever the instruction on scientific and literary themes can be of such a character as to afford the opportunity of confirming the Christian faith, and strengthening Christian purposes, it should in all cases be given. If it furnishes no such opportunity, the character of the instructor may still attract and influence his pupils. Those who found and endow Christian colleges may as properly endow them for purposes of religious culture, so far as such culture can be successfully applied, as make them places of intellectual discipline. Those who do not accept the Christian notion of character, who do not believe in Christ as the object of man's confidence and the light and hope of his life, may see no propriety in connecting these influences with his training in youth. They would exclude religion and Christianity from the college for the same reasons and no other for which they would exclude them from the conduct of the life. Conversely, the same reasoning which would exclude them from a place in the college, would require that they be rejected altogether.

Fourth.—If moral and religious perfection are the end of all education, then moral and religious culture are friendly to education and culture of every kind. " The end of learning," says Milton, " is to repair the ruins of our first parents, by regaining to know God aright, and out of that knowledge to love him, to imitate him, to be like him, as we may the nearest by possessing our souls of true virtue, which being united to the heavenly grace of faith, makes up the highest perfection. But because our understanding cannot in this body found itself but on sensible things, nor arrive so clearly to the knowledge of God and invisible things, as by orderly conning over the visible and inferior creatures, the same method is necessarily to be followed in all discreet teaching." These views, with some qualifications of phraseology, will be accepted by all those who have any faith or interest in religious truth. They are in brief " that moral and religious perfection are the final aim of all human culture, as they are of our existence and discipline in the human condition. This end is promoted by education, chiefly by the study of nature and of books." Now the question upon which opinions differ, is, whether this final, that is the religious aim, ought to be distinctly recognized in our educational arrangements, especially in the higher institutions of learning. Some contend that any recognition of religious ends other than the most indirect and incidental must interfere with the direct object of education, which is culture, and in this way may defeat the ends of religion itself. Others contend, that inasmuch as religion is supreme, it should be recognized and pursued in the college, even at the expense and sacrifice of culture ; that whatever else should be sacrificed even in an institution professedly devoted to education, religion should be regarded as supreme. We contend that there is no incompatibility between the two ; that while culture should be made the direct object of every institution of learning, and in one sense the immediate aim of its arrangements, this aim is not hindered but promoted by that enlightened recognition of religion which culture makes possible. We hold that religion controls and tempers culture, in order to stimulate, refine, and elevate it ; and culture, in its turn, enlightens and liberalizes religion. We do not agree with Matthew Arnold in his *Culture and Anarchy*, that the Christian element is essentially " Hebraistic" in the sense of being dogmatic, narrow, and intolerant, and that as such it is opposed to the " Hellenistic" element, which is reflecting, enlightened, tolerant, and civilized. Rather do we hold that Christianity mediates between Judaism and Hellenism, that it is Hebraism Hellenized, and contains in itself the excellences of both directions, softening the austerities of Judaism by the refinements of Greece, and thus enlarging its narrowness by " turning a stream of fresh and free thought upon our stock notions and habits." Or rather we should say that it is only by the touch of the divinely human Master and Lord of Christianity, that these antagonistic elements can be fused into something nobler than either, the self-sacrifice and worship of that Christian love which " seeketh not her own.", Did we not believe that an earnest and spiritual Christianity is compatible with and favorable to the highest forms of human culture, we should not believe it to be from God. But believing that it is divine, not merely in its moral and religious relations to the individual soul, but in its adaptations to every possible development of humanity, we think that its truths and spirit should be distinctly and prominently recognized in all our higher institutions of learning ; and this not merely from its acknowledged importance and supremacy, but because of its beneficent influence upon learning and culture themselves. We would not make of our colleges houses of piety as such, we would not

turn their scholastic exercises into spiritual *retraites ;*
we would not lower the standard of learning or diminish the requirements of taste and culture ; but we would
distinctly hold up and exemplify the most spiritual and
earnest forms of Christian duty and the Christian life,
as the ends to which all learning and all culture should
be consecrated as supreme. The mottoes upon the
seals of Harvard and Yale respectively, when united
into one, happily express our own opinion, as they do
justice to the claims of religion on the one hand, and of
culture on the other. Harvard, in her *Christo et Eccle-
siæ,* pays the chief homage to religion, as it was natural
that she should, being older in time. Yale completes
the motto, by *Lux et Veritas*, providing for culture in
words that remind us of Arnold's oft-repeated " sweetness and light."

We trust that none of our readers will be surprised
that we assert, that *other things being equal*,—as endowments, time, access to an intelligent and refined
community, with the appliances with which such a
community provides itself,—that institution of learning
which is earnestly religious is certain to make the largest and most valuable achievements in science and
learning, as well as in literary tastes and capacity.

Among the particulars in which an earnest Christian
spirit is fitted to act favorably upon the culture of the
colleges, are the following. It is favorable to persevering *industry*. Culture of every sort is the fruit of application. Success in any science and art is achieved
by labor. The spirit of Christianity is a spirit of self-
denying and patient service. To what feats of literary
work has it not prompted, in the amazing toil by day

and night, through month and years, which has wrought
the ponderous tomes that fill the libraries of the
learned? It is true other motives prompt to laborious
erudition and scientific toil; the motives of ambition
in all its forms, and sometimes those of malevolent passion or critical spleen, but none of these is a force
which in its nature is so tense and untiring as are religious duty and Christian self-denial. What superhu-
man patience has been shown by the devotees of
Christian art in all its forms, who have labored, not
merely for an immortality of earthly fame, but under
the inspiration which came from the assured hope of a
personal immortality which should surpass by its satisfying realities their loftiest ideals !

The Christian spirit is in its nature *truth-loving*. If
there is any one feature prominent in the character of
its great Founder, in which he was before his own time
and has given character to all the time that has followed, it is his recognition of the independence of the
truth as such, and of its authority, by virtue of its hold
upon the reason. If there is any one spirit which he
has inculcated by precept and example, it is the spirit
of brave allegiance to truth. If any duty may be said
to have been prominently recognized and enforced by
him, it is the duty of candor in weighing all sorts of
evidence. The father of the inductive philosophy could
give no better illustration of the spirit which he regarded
as the condition of successful investigation and of actual
progress, than in these words, " that it is no less true in
this human kingdom of knowledge, than in God's kingdom of heaven, that no man shall enter it *except he become first as a little child.*" It enjoins the love of all

sorts of truth—Truth of art and literature, as well as of that beauty which is but another name for æsthetic truth. The precept " whatsoever things are true, whatsoever things are lovely, whatsoever things are of good report, *think on these things*," provides for the most catholic taste conceivable, for the most progressive civilization, for all true refinement in art, in literature, in manners, and in civilization of every kind. It not only provides for all these, but it enjoins them all as duties.

It is, moreover, *refining* in its operation and influences, and so far is eminently favorable to culture. It represses the animal passions with the spiritual debasement which they involve. It rises above mere worldly tendencies ; with their inevitably hardening tendency, however brilliant the polish of which this hardness is capable. It substitutes for this the more delicate graces of spiritual modesty and spiritual aspirations. It destroys the selfish affections and introduces in their place a love which is warm as well as ennobling. It rises above the envious jealousies which, if reports are true, do sometimes separate scientists, poets, and musicians—as well as theologians and religionists. In short, the indirect effect of Christian feeling is to call forth and encourage whatever in human sensibility is of finer texture, and to keep it fresh and pure. The same Christian faith which, when it enters a cottage, other things being equal, awakens and intensifies the love of flowers, of music, of poetry, and of pictures, does also, when it dominates in the cultured soul, increase the delicacy and enlarge the sphere of its tastes. By the same rule, when it prevails in a university it tends to make its members more refined in all their capacities

10

for æsthetic progress, as well as quickens the desire to exercise and perfect them.

We do not contend that Christianity is the same thing as culture, or that Christian attainments may be accepted in a college as an equivalent for attainments in science and literature. As we have said, the university and the college are not proximately designed for religious culture and spiritual edification, but for study and intellectual discipline. To turn them into houses of religion or to use them chiefly or prominently as places for spiritual instead of intellectual exercises, is grossly to pervert them, and like all other perversions and half-truths is to foster all manner of spiritual monstrosities ; as hypocrisy, cant, spiritual pride, asceticism, and the like. Hence we do not care to see the religious features of a college paraded in the newspapers, or the reports of its religious condition and doings made the subject of ostentatious comments. The impropriety in such cases is eminently conspicuous and offensive, because it is an offense against religion and culture combined. Pharisaism and cant are never in good taste.

We cannot deny that Christianity sometimes seems to be antagonistic to culture, especially to culture in its higher forms. Its ethical claims are supreme and uncompromising. It sets the moral excellence which comes of its faith and obedience, far above all other excellences and requires its disciples to esteem all these as nothing in this comparison. It requires that whenever a question arises between the gratification of a taste and the discharge of a duty, or between the culture of the intellect and the culture of the heart, the former should be sacrificed. All tastes and all enjoyments, which pertain to the present, must be held as secondary to those which pertain to the higher and unseen life. Hence it has been inferred by the detractors of Christianity, that it is barbarous because it does not exalt art and culture as supreme ; they forgetting that the nature or fate which they set up in the place of Christ is equally inexorable and cruel, when it burns, and deforms, and drowns, or limits, in myriads of ways, the works and aspirations of culture and art. It has also been inferred by those of its friends, who are narrow in their understanding of Christianity or who make it a cloak for envy or suspicion toward those whose tastes are more refined than their own, that while a certain degree of knowledge and culture are enforced by Christianity, any excess beyond is inconsistent with its spirit. For these and other reasons the impression has prevailed that it is unfriendly to eminent attainments in science and letters, and therefore cannot be comfortably housed in a university which would stand at the front of modern achievements.

To shut off any such unfortunate and unwarrantable inferences, we concede that Christianity has much to learn from culture ; that while it is refining in its influences and therefore tends to culture, it is itself refined and enlarged by the learning to which, in its essential nature, it is altogether friendly. Culture as such largely pertains to the expression of that character of which Christianity is the spring. Grace and perfection of manners, purity and felicitousness of diction, dexterity in the accomplishments of music, drawing, and painting, or nicety of sense in the judgment of the same, as well as skill and science in the more intellectual departments,

all confer upon Christianity the means of more perfectly manifesting the power of its spiritual beauty, and
teach Christianity itself how to become more attractive
by assuming those adornments which she herself has
very largely created, and all of which she welcomes
and rejoices in as appropriate to herself.

But while we concede all this, and even contend that
Christianity may learn from culture, we contend also
that culture itself is exposed to certain excesses, for
which Christianity is the only adequate counterpoise
and remedy. We affirm that a vigorous religious influence is needed in every university, if for no other reason, simply as a corrective against the one-sidedness,
—the Philistinism we might call it, of modern science
and literature.

Modern culture, from the very perfection which it requires and attains in particular departments, tends to
narrowness, positiveness, and conceit. The devotee of
any single branch of knowledge or department of art
must devote himself exclusively and perseveringly to
his chosen profession. His zeal is usually proportioned to his success, and his enthusiasm confines his
attention more and more exclusively to the objects and
pursuits of his limited sphere. He becomes great in a
single department, because his mind moves within that
alone. It often happens that while he is strong in one
direction, he is weak in thought and opinion with respect to every other. But it does not follow because he
is weak and even ignorant, that he is sensible of his defects and incapacity. On the contrary, his conscious
superiority in his chosen pursuit, makes him positive,
dogmatic, and conceited in respect to every other.

Hence the sectarian narrowness which divides the devotees of the physical sciences, and their acknowledged proneness to cliques which is recognized in the pointed words of President White: " It may seem strange that this should be alluded to ; but in view of the fact that more than one American college has been ruined by such feuds, and that very many have been crippled ; in view of the cognate fact that the *odium theologicum* seems now outdone by hates between scientific cliques and dogmas ; that as a rule it is now impossible to receive an impartial opinion from one scientific man respecting another ; and that these gentlemen, in their jealousies and likenings, are evidently awaiting some one with a spark of the *Molière* genius, to cover them before the country with ridicule and contempt, we do not think that the Board is likely to give too much importance to this." (*Report, etc., on the Organization of Cornell University.*)

It may seem to some a little strange that we suggest that Christian science furnishes the natural and most efficient prophylactic and cure for these sectarian narrownesses and embitterments. The study of God in his relations to what is known or knowable in the universe of spirit and matter certainly forces to a general consideration of what is known or knowable in the several departments of science. It requires the consideration, superficial indeed but respectful, of the principles and authority of every one of the sciences. It forces each expert to look beyond the narrow bounds of his own speciality, and to see how it adjusts itself to its neighbor. It now and then carries him up to a point of view which overlooks the limits of the special sciences, that he may see how they all adjust themselves to that underlying philosophy, which recognizes in some sort their bond of unity—whether this bond is called the Absolute of the schools, or the living God of the people. In this way Theology becomes, not merely in the language of Bacon the "haven and Sabbath of all man's contemplations," but in a certain sense the *commune vinculum* of the special sciences. It is such, so far as it forces the devotee of each to look beyond the limits of his own field, and to recognize the existence and rights of his neighbors. It even becomes a harmonizing and purifying power, so far as it liberalizes the mind of each narrow devotee, by lifting his thoughts now and then up to God, and forcing him to recognize the relations of his own science to Him. Even if Theology is not cultivated as a science, but is present to the individual scientist and the scientific community only so far as is required for religious faith and feeling, it must still quicken and widen their intellects, and enable them to pursue their special departments in a spirit less narrow and more catholic. Should it be urged that Theology, in its turn, is jealous of scientific progress, and hostile to its freedom, we have no occasion to affirm or deny that it may be. All that we contend for is that the influence of Christian theology and of Christian faith upon the professed devotees of science themselves, legitimately tends to make them more profound, and therefore more broad and catholic as philosophers. So far as observation or history has taught us, Christian Geologists, Chemists, Philosophers, and Historians have not loved scientific truth as truth any the less purely, or followed it any the less boldly or bravely than those who were not Christian. Nor have they, when other things were equal been a whit less diligent, earnest, and successful, than those who have accepted none of the so-called "theological dogmas or Christian traditions." We venture to affirm, that when other things were equal they have been, in every respect, better philosophers for being also "theologians;" more broad and more profound in their intellectual activities and achievements, and immeasurably more noble and generous in their tempers as teachers and writers, and in the intercourse of science and of life.

Faraday was no less enlightened and broad-minded as a chemical philosopher because he kept his Christian faith warm and true in the humblest fashion. *Alexander Humboldt* would have been wider-minded, and larger-hearted as a thinker, had he not so timidly shunned those religious avowals and religious sympathies, which his brother William so freely expressed. "They that deny a God, destroy man's nobility," says Bacon, and Atheism never fails to develop something of the ignoble, whether in the school, the saloon, or the beer-shop. No Atheistic theory or Pantheistic philosophy was ever intellectually great, or æsthetically noble. The mark of intellectual narrowness and conceit will be ineffaceably set upon any college or school of science of which the prevailing spirit is godless or anti-Christian.

The question is not, as many would represent it to be, a question between the interests of theology and religion on the one hand and the interests of scientific culture on the other, but it is a question between the most efficient methods of advancing both science and culture. We contend, for the reasons already given,

that a religious college will, in the long run, if all else
is equal, do more for science and culture than the college which sets aside or makes little of religious influence and of Christian truth. Nor is it a question
whether science shall be free and be pursued in a liberal spirit, or whether it shall be constrained by theological prepossessions and be limited by Christian dogmas and the Christian history. We contend that the
Christian investigator is pledged by the very spirit of
his system to be a bold and fearless follower of the
truth wherever the truth shall lead, even though it
should lead him to the rejection of any part or the
whole of the Christian history and theology. It is simply whether true culture can be effectually received
without moral culture, and whether moral culture can
be effectually enforced without religious motives, and
whether in a community which is in a condition of eminent exposure as well as of especial promise, Christian
influences ought not to be employed with the utmost
possible efficiency.

Fifth.—Religious influences and religious teaching
should be employed in colleges, in order to exclude
and counteract the atheistic tendencies of much of
modern science, literature, and culture.

We have already alluded to the advantage which science and culture receive when they are truly Christian.
We cannot overlook the fact that not a little of science
and culture at present is conspicuously anti-Christian.
Under whatever name this exclusion of Christianity is
known or under whatever covering it may hide itself, its
existence and its presence can neither be disguised nor
denied. Indeed, science in many of its forms does and

must, as science, take a position which is theistic or anti-theistic, that is, which in principle is supernatural or anti-supernatural; which either includes or excludes religious faith and worship. In much of the teaching that is appropriate to the college, scientific positions must be taken which, by logical necessity, lead to the one or the other of these consequences. Every educated man now-a-days must either accept or reject the ill-disguised materialism of *Huxley*, the cerebralism of *Bain*, the thin and vacillating metaphysics of *Mill*, the evolutionism of *Herbert Spencer*, with its demonstrated impossibility of a positive theism, or the confident but superficial fatalism of the devotees of Nature or the Absolute. In History every man must take or reject the atheistic fatalism of *Buckle*. In Literature, every one must accept or reject the worship of Genius, or the worship of God ; the self-centered adoration of self-development, or the generous self-forgetfulness that has made heroes and martyrs ; the imitation of *Goethe*, in his contentment with the present, and his cool submission to fate, or of those Christian poets and critics who have been discontented with the best of earth, because of their ardent out-reaching to what is promised in the future life. There are, we know, multitudes of cultured youth who seek to evade the necessity of adopting either of these antagonistic theories of faith and of life, under the impression that true opinions and fixed opinions were never so hard as now to be reached, that philosophy, and literature, and theology each require and sanction uncertainty of decision and protracted inquiry, and that so much can be said for each of these opposing sides, that he must be a nar-

row and audacious man who decides and acts too soon.
The plea of freedom and tolerance is put in on every
quarter, and the dignity and duty of positive opinions
earnestly held is too generally lost sight of among men
of the most refined tastes, and the loftiest aspirations.
To yield to this solicitation is for the time, to be practically materialistic, atheistic, and un-Christian, and the
fashion of the times in certain circles of educated young
men, sets strongly in this direction.   Least and last of
all, would we have our colleges countenance or yield to
su:h a fashion !   If the higher institutions of learning
take an indifferent position with respect to their influence, that position must be practically a negative position.   If for fear of losing patronage, or in order to
seem to be tolerant and just, they shall abstain from
exerting any positive religious influence, they must abstain altogether from teaching physiology, psychology,
metaphysics, morals, history, and literature, for all of
these do involve what is called a theological bias, either
positive or negative, in whatever way they may be
taught.   The question is not whether the college shall,
or shall not, teach theology, but what theology it shall
teach,—theology according to Comte and Spencer, or
according to Bacon and Christ, theology according to
Moses and Paul, or according to Buckle and Draper.
For a college to hesitate to teach theism and Christianity is practically to proclaim that in the opinion of
its guardians and teachers the evidence for and against,
is so evenly balanced that it would be unfair for them to
throw their influence on either side ; and is in fact to
throw it on the side of materialism, fatalism, or atheism.
    Such a position, under whatever fair pretences it is

taken, we hold to be not only dangerous to the community in the present crisis of opinion, but to be fearfully and fatally criminal. We assume that the guardians and patrons of every college in this country are in the very largest proportion positively and earnestly theistic and Christian in their own faith. It is their privilege and their duty to use the means within their own hands to arrest and stem the tendency to atheism and anti-christianism which we have described. They are bound to do this, not merely as theists and as Christians, but as the friends of science and culture. This they can do, as we shall show, without departing in the least from the utmost respect to the private judgment of their pupils, and without incurring the reproach or arousing the suspicion of sectarianism or bigotry. It is surely competent for the guardians of these colleges to judge whether the men whom they select are or are not possessed of the tolerance and tact which may be required to avoid reasonable occasions of offense. If all classes of opinions should have a hearing, as they ought, let theistic teachers be selected who will represent fairly all the atheistic and anti-Christian objections and difficulties, but let not atheism or anti-Christianity be taught in any college chairs, either directly or indirectly, either in the form of philosophy or theology, or in the guise of history, literature, or criticism. To claim that these forms of opinion have a right to be heard is to claim that any one of the so-called American public, or any score, have an inalienable right that any shade of opinion which he or they may hold, should be held and taught from some one of the chairs of every college.

We would distinguish here between the college and the university. The disposition to confound the two is perpetually appearing at every turn of this discussion, and at every step of our progress, not merely as involving an intellectual fallacy of the *ambiguous middle*, but the practical error of prescribing a course of instruction for boys which is only suitable for men. The college is a training place for minds that are yet immature in the elements of knowledge and culture. The university is a teaching place for those who are supposed to have been trained to the capacities and responsibilities of incipient manhood. Whatever freedom may be claimed for the university in teaching and learning, does not sanction a similar freedom in the college. We are not prepared to allow, that even in the university every shade of opinion should have an advocate, under the countenance of its guardians, and with the sanction of their consent. While we would defend to the last degree the tolerance of free speech and free discussion, and would enforce with the utmost scrupulousness the courtesies of fair and dispassionate controversy, we are not required by these duties to set in the chair of authorized teaching, even in a free university, the representatives of every shade of literary opinion, or of anti-religious philosophy. We acknowledge it is not always easy to apply these general principles. It is not easy to say how far a man's philosophical or religious creed should be considered as an objection to his holding a college or university chair, but the principle holds good that at whatever sacrifice, the college at least should maintain a positive religious influence and character, whatever freedom may be allowed in the university.

President Eliot has touched upon this subject in his Inaugural Address somewhat more daintily than upon many other topics. We accept without reserve his remark, that "the word education is a standing protest against dogmatic teaching," whatever subject matter is taught. The President limits this observation to what he calls "philosophical subjects." We would apply it with equal freedom to the science of Theology and even to the inculcation of religious truth in colleges. With some qualification, we find a most important truth in the following sentence : " The notion that education consists in the authoritative inculcation of what the teacher deems true may be logical and appropriate in a convent, or a seminary for priests, but it is intolerable in universities and public schools from primary to professional." It is one thing, however, for a college or a university to teach by "authoritative inculcation" and altogether another thing for either to assume in its teachings and in the selection of text books and teachers, that some truths, scientific, historic and religious are to be regarded as established and permanent. We presume that President Eliot would have the university both presume and assume that the Newtonian system is true rather than the Ptolemaic. Possibly, he would go further and have it accept as axiomatic the rather recent and as yet not undisputed doctrines of the Correlation of forces and the Conservation of force. Doubtless he would proceed upon the assumption that the axioms and demonstrations of the common geometry are trustworthy, though different philosophers still prosecute their opposing, and in some cases, " bottomless speculations " in respect to both. He would also

accept the methods of induction, although Kant would
make the principles which underlie them the outgrowth
of forms of thought having simply subjective validity, and
J. S. Mill would make them the products of "inseparable associations," and Herbert Spencer, brain growths
that have been evolved by a long continued course of dif-
ferentiation and integration, and have been transmitted
by hereditary propagation.   Surely it is not dogmatic, to
assume in the same sense and for the practical direction
of our teaching, that the Christian theism, and the Christian history, and the Christian ethics are still "in force"
and that they are likely to be permanent, and in this
belief to consecrate to Christ and the Church a university designed for liberal teaching.   We may presume
that President Eliot means something of the sort in the
rather equivocal observation that "the student should
be shown what is *still in force* of institutions or philo-
sophies mainly outgrown."   If the Christian theism,
the Christian ethics, the Christian history, and the
Christian civilization may be allowed that recognition
in the instructions and arrangements of any university
which is accorded to the Newtonian system and the
Baconian induction, there will be no question that that
"university in our day serves Christ and the Church."
It cannot be objected that ethical and Christian science
are to be excepted because they rest on "bottomless
speculations" by any one who is aware that the nature
of matter and of spirit as well as the fundamental principles of mathematics and of all scientific processes
and results are variously defined and defended in
the speculations of those who none the less agree in
the conviction that they are established facts and

truths. We agree most cordially with President Eliot that : " The worthy fruit of academic culture is an open mind, trained to careful thinking, instructed in the methods of philosophic investigation, acquainted in a general way with the accumulated thought of past generations and penetrated with humility. It is thus that the university in our day serves Christ and the Church." *Thus*, indeed ; but not *only thus ;* for the reasons already given. Why it may and should do more, we need not explain a second time.

These thoughts lead us to our next inquiry, by what means can the colleges maintain a religious character ? What methods of influence may be employed ? and within what limits may these be applied ? We cannot, as we have just suggested, be required to discuss or to answer these and the like questions any more than when we lay down positive fundamental principles and rules of duty, we can anticipate all the refinements of casuistry. The following duties are clear. The college should maintain public Christian worship, and this should be conducted in an earnest and positive manner. It should give positive Christian instruction concerning the evidence and truths of theism and Christianity. It should by the influence and activities of its teachers favor an active Christian life. It should pervade all the teaching which admits it with a distinct and earnest recognition of Christian truth. At the same time, as we have already explained, the college is professedly and primarily a place for intellectual culture. To intellectual culture the chief energies of instructors and pupils should be given. All the conditions required for successful study should be furnished. Among these are

prominent, perfect tolerance of every form of religious
opinion, encouragement to the utmost freedom of reading and inquiry, and the inculcation of the bravest confidence in the authority of evidence, and the application
of a critical judgment.

The point of the greatest delicacy is one in respect
to which no fixed rules can be established, and that is
how far the religious opinions and character of a person
son should be considered in estimating his qualifications for the post of teacher. Such a question as this
cannot be settled in a general way, or by prescribed
formulæ. There are manifold peculiarities of personal
character, besides erudition or even aptness to teach,
which render an individual a very suitable or a very
unsuitable member of a college faculty. There are
many well instructed, and very eminent men, who are
withal very earnest religionists, who by the very indis-
cretion and overplus of their zeal, are totally disquali-
fied for a place in a college. There are men, on the
other hand, the sensitiveness of whose conscience, and
the hesitation of whose temper, make their "inquiring
spirit" and their "honest doubts" express infinitely
more of religious earnestness and of religious power,
than the plump and unhesitating orthodoxy of many a
coarse-minded and hard favored dogmatist. There are
some chairs the instruction of which cannot be greatly
affected by the faith or the character of the incumbent.
There are other chairs, which an anti-Christian sophist
or a velvet-footed infidel might pervert to the most disastrous uses. If the principle and duty be acknowledged for which we contend, the application may be
safely entrusted to the wise discretion of those whose
business it is to decide upon individual cases.

Against the view which we have taken, manifold objections may be offered. One of the most formidable is, that if the colleges are positively religious institutions, they must be necessarily sectarian. This does not follow. A sectarian or denominational college is a college conducted with reference to the interests of a single denomination. Its distinctive doctrines, its forms of worship, its peculiar religious spirit, are all made prominent, as fundamentally Christian, as alone authorized, or as preëminently excellent. Such colleges may sometimes be needed for the *prestige* of the denomination, or to guard its youth against being drawn from its fold. The lamentable and unjustifiable divisions among Christians may therefore involve the necessity of a few colleges that are distinctively and avowedly sectarian. But the foundation or the conducting of a college in the interests of a single denomination has not generally been successful, for the reason that the culture which colleges impart is, in its nature, liberalizing ; and that to Christian earnestness, when instructed by Christian learning, the exclusiveness of any Protestant sect becomes almost invariably distasteful. Just in proportion as the college becomes eminent in its culture, just in that proportion does it lose sight of any single sect and denomination, and take into its larger view the common relations of all to culture and to Christ. A truly religious college cannot, in our opinion, be eminently sectarian, and yet be true to its appropriate function, by yielding itself to the influence of the science, art, and culture which it is appointed to promote. However strictly it may be held by its charter to the name or the organization of any single denomination, it will outgrow all narrowing relations to it, or make its denomination outgrow them, just as fast as it grows at all.

If this be so, then why should it be attached to any one denomination,—why should it not be the common property of many, or the common property of none? We reply, a college in which several denominations have a partial interest, will inevitably be divided and dishonored by ignoble sectarian strifes. The several denominations which hold it in common will regard each other with that "eternal vigilance" which in such cases easily degenerates into perpetual suspicion ; its officers will be elected, and its policy will be determined, with a judgment divided between the interests of the college and the interests of the sect. Some of the most disgraceful exhibitions of sectarian wrangling and craft of a religious sort that this country has ever witnessed, have occurred in the history of colleges which have been the joint property of two or three denominations.

But why not let them be the property of none? This can only happen as the board of trust and management is made up partially or wholly of members who have no religious preferences at all. Or why not solve the problem by throwing the college upon the endowments and the care of the State? The objection to either of these arrangements, so far as the religious relations and character of the college is concerned, is that it will immediately become the object of the ambition, or the victim of the strife of some one or more religious sects, with the never ending discussions which must inevitably follow ; or it will have no religious character at all. In the present divided condition of Christendom, there seems to be no solution of the problem, except the one which has been accepted in this country, viz., that the college should be in the hands of some single religious denomination, in order to secure unity and effect to its religious character and influence, and that it should be preserved from sectarian bias and illiberality, by its responsibility to the community which it would influence, and the enlightened and catholic influences of the culture to which it is devoted.

We see no alternative between this and the abandonment of any special and efficient religious influence *i. e.*, the complete secularization of the college. For this alternative many leading minds are already prepared ; more than are ready to acknowledge. There are not a few who contrast what they call the *people's colleges*, or the *State colleges*, with what they choose to designate as *sectarian colleges*, to the disadvantage of the latter,— who do not desire that the college should have any positively Christian influence, either because they do not believe it has any place there, or because they would attract students from those who have no positive religious faith for themselves, or desire none for their children. That these views are incorrect we have endeavored to prove, by our argument. We have only to add, that as between terms of reproach, if *sectarian* is fairly charged on the one side, *godless* may be as fairly retorted on the other, and if a purely secular college will attract a certain portion of the community, positively religious colleges will attract another. If the two sorts of colleges are fairly tried, the fruits of the two will be made manifest. It will be seen after a generation, whether Christianized science, art, and litera-

ture, has any advantage over that which is un-Christian
or non-Christian ; whether the education and culture
that are elevated by the Christian faith, have any advantage over those which are secular and atheistic.   One
thing is certain, that all the experiments which have
been tried in this country to conduct institutions of
learning without Christian worship and Christian influences, have failed ; that all the so-called State colleges
have, in some sort, been forced to adopt, either directly
or indirectly, the same methods of religious influence
which are employed in the Christian colleges ; that in
the choice of their officers, they have largely given the
preference to men of positive and earnest Christian
faith, for their greater usefulness as teachers, and their
greater acceptableness to the community.   Those who
believe that the Christian argument has been nearly exhausted, or that the Christian history has been demonstrated to be impossible, and must be regarded as practically false,—that the Christ of the New Testament is
but a human idea, with no personal authority, will of
course, in the light of their advanced opinions, be willing to repeat the experiment under what they consider
more favorable auspices, but they cannot ask those to
believe in its success, who hold another theory of religion and Christianity.

Those who believe that Christian truth and the
Christian history are divine in their origin and permanent in their influence will do well to remember, that a
Christian college must be amply provided with all the
appliances of Science and Literature in order to be efficient and successful in the service of either Christianity or culture.   Its scholarship must be varied and
profound.   The several departments of knowledge must

be represented by able men. Its Libraries must be replenished with the stores of the oldest learning and the contributions of recent research and speculation. The spirit of every such college should be catholic, liberal, and tolerant, while it should be believing, devout, and fervent. The culture which it imparts should be in no respect inferior to that which the country or the times demand. The friends of Christianity very readily acknowledge the obligation to provide institutions of learning for the service of the Christian Church. They are not always aware that the duty is equally incumbent to place the institutions in the foremost rank in respect to the thoroughness and perfection of the culture which they impart.

XII.

THE GUARDIANSHIP AND CONTROL OF THE COLLEGE.

We are reminded here of another topic which has been more or less distinctly discussed by and before the American public—*whether the instruction and government of the American colleges have not been too largely intrusted to clergymen ?* Clergymen, it is said, must, by the very nature and influence of their profession, be essentially artificial and one-sided. They cannot and they ought not to be " men of the world" in the good sense of the phrase, that is, they cannot judge of men as they are, with fairness and discrimination, for the reason that all men present themselves to their view in constrained attitudes and under artificial lights, and they in their turn must look at men through highly refracting media. They usually want tact and delicacy in the management of men. They do not approach them with that skill which can only be acquired by a large experience under a great variety of circumstances. They are also not usually good men of business, and ought, therefore, not to be intrusted with ·the investment and care of the large sums of money which are required for the support of a college. They are not familiar with the advancements of modern science, and unlikely to be abreast with the culture which is required by the present generation. For these and other reasons it is urged that they ought not to constitute so large a portion of the boards of instruction and management as they have done in the majority of our colleges.

We are not prepared to assert that in some cases there is not reason for these criticisms. But we can assert with considerable confidence that it would be difficult to show in any individual case that where clergymen have failed, either as members of a college faculty or of a board of trustees, layman would have succeeded. The relation of one of these boards to the other is so different in different colleges that it is almost impossible to reason from failure or success in one case to failure or success in another. In some colleges the faculty have little influence in the policy and appointments. In others one or two individuals, either lay or clerical, very largely determine both. The success or failure of many institutions seems to be occasioned by excellences or defects which are individual rather than professional.

There are several obvious reasons, however, why clergymen have been, and must still continne to be, intrusted very largely with duties and responsibilities of this kind. In the first place, most of the colleges have originated in the most thankless and self-sacrificing services. To services of this kind clergymen are consecrated by the vows and the spirit of their profession. The labor, self-denial, and disinterested toil which have been required to lay the foundations and rear the superstructure of the most successful colleges of this country cannot be too easily estimated. To a very large extent these have been endured and rendered by clergymen. The care, inquiry, invention, and correspondence, the personal toil and sacrifice which devolve upon those who act as trustees of an infant and often of a well-established college are such that few persons except clergymen are willing to undertake them. Clergymen may not always be good men of business, but they generally know who are such, and have generally the good sense and good feeling to ask the advice and to defer to the decisions of those who are, which is more than can always be said of laymen who are called to duties and trusts to which they are not competent. Hence, with the best intentions and with far greater experience in affairs generally, laymen may fail where clergymen succeed. As to defect of tact or power of adaptation, especially in the management of men, an excess of tact has not unfrequently been charged upon the clergy. Clerical art and finesse have in not a few cases become proverbial as grounds of reproach.

Clergymen are far more commonly interested in matters of education than laymen, by reason of a certain breadth of culture and generosity of disposition which are the results of Christian science. Though the *idola tribus* may exact from them a devotion which is sometimes narrow and exclusive, yet their profession is from its very nature, as we have shown, the most liberalizing of all, from the common relation it involves to other branches of knowledge and from the habit of seeking for the foundations of truth which the study of God and religion induces. It is but the simple truth to say that there is many a country clergyman, whose income is counted by hundreds where that of his classmate lawyer and judge is counted by thousands, who knows incalculably more of science as such, and of the way to learn and to teach it than the aforesaid judge or lawyer whose reputation is the very highest in his profession. The professional studies of the clergyman do also very emphatically involve and cultivate a sympathy with literature of all kinds. The practice of composition and of public speaking upon elevated themes, involves more or less interest in the study of language and in works of imaginative literature. The clergy as such have, at least in this country, a more pronounced and catholic literary taste than the members of any other profession. They constitute, indeed, to a very large extent, the literary class—the class who furnish most frequently public addresses, essays, reviews, and pamphlets. Educated lawyers, physicians, and merchants write very little in comparison with them, and are much less frequently readers beyond the range of their own profession.

The reason why clergymen are so generally selected as professors and teachers in colleges, is two-fold : First, that the men best qualified by special culture are oftener found in the clerical profession ; and, second, that the profession of teaching is akin to that of the clergyman in the smallness of its pay and the unselfish patience which it involves. At the same time it is not usually true, so far as we have observed, that there is not a sufficiently large number of laymen in the faculties and boards of trust to correct the one-sidedness and to supplement the defects of their clerical colleagues. We have never observed that there was in such boards any jealousy of lay coöperation, any disposition to foster a clerical spirit or any one-sided results from clerical supervision. The cloistered, scholastic, and pedantic influences of the college which are some-

11

times complained of, so far as there are any, usually
proceed from lay professors, who have never known
anything but a scholar's life. The *doctores umbratiles* of
the American colleges are not infrequently laymen.

The relations of the colleges to the community are those
of partially endowed *beneficent institutions*, which are designed to confer important benefits upon the young.
For the faithful and successful discharge of their duties,
the instructors are directly responsible to the managers or trustees, and both are indirectly responsible
to the public. Many of the beneficent results which
these institutions propose to accomplish are not immediately obvious. The adaptation of the means to the
ends proposed is not always easy to be seen, and
as a general rule can be judged and estimated only by
a few. When the results do not seem to be the best
conceivable, it is not always easy to say whether any
other training or appliances would have wrought results
so good. The training of an individual youth in a liberal spirit to the capacity and the desire to be a useful
public man, either in the exercise of a profession or in
any leading position, is a matter concerning which the
experience of the past should be most cautiously regarded. It should be committed to enterprising men,
indeed, who are not afraid of innovation or reform, but
who are also far-seeing, thoughtful, and self-relying.
Extemporaneous and flippant dogmatism and ambitious and satirical criticism by bold adventurers or uncultivated Philistines are especially out of place in discussions concerning such trusts or the persons who
manage them. They do not deserve to be heeded except for their power to mislead the confiding public.

Though, in one sense, the managers of colleges need not ask the advice of the public, because they know and understand, better than the public can, the duties with which they are intrusted ; yet, in another sense, they ought never to forget that, if they do not retain the confidence of the public, it will be impossible for them to be of service to the public.   If the community does not value the training and the instruction which they give, they cannot benefit it, and they might as well not exist.   And yet, as we have observed, the public are not competent to judge directly of many, not to say of most, of the questions which are to be decided.

It is most fortunate that, under these circumstances, the colleges have always had one resource.   They have usually been able to rely upon their own graduates. These act as *internuncii* between the colleges and the public whenever there is occasion for explanation or danger of misunderstanding.   In times of a conflict between the two, the alumni of a powerful college are, indeed, as " arrows in the hand of a mighty man." " Happy is the ' college' that hath its quiver full of them ; *they shall speak with the enemies in the gate.*" The graduates of the American colleges are their glory and their strength.   They are their *glory*, so far as they show, by mental power, by varied acquirements, and accomplished culture, what their *Alma Mater* has done for them, either by her unwelcome restraints and hard duties, or by those influences that were more genial in their operation and are more delightful in the remembrance.   They are their *strength*, so far as they are distinctly conscious of the benefits which they derived from the college, and are forward to acknowledge them.

The colleges of this country have nothing to fear, so long as the majority of their pupils continue to confide in their systems of discipline and instruction, and in the men who administer them. While it is true that colleges and universities, all the world over, are objects of special regard to those whom they have trained, the colleges of America have the strongest conceivable hold upon the affections of their pupils, from the strength of the associations which are here fixed and interwoven, as well as from the sense of the value of the discipline here received. These alumni, it is true, retain and somewhat liberally exercise the traditional privileges of all children, freely to criticise the ways of the house-hold. They retain vivid recollections of the tedium of many of the college tasks, and the unwelcome charac-ter of some of its discipline. Nor do they always weigh the import of what they say, or are they always entirely confident of the justice of the criticisms which they un-thinkingly utter. Sometimes their fault-finding is but the result of their jealous regard for the honor of their college and an indirect expression of the fervor of their zeal for its more abundant prosperity.

The alumni are greatly mistaken if they ever suppose that the trustees or faculty are indifferent to their good opinion, or delight to trifle with it. This good opinion they are not only most desirous to gain, but they are sensible that if they lose it they must lose their hold upon the public at large. At the same time, as honest men, they will be more anxious to deserve than to gain their favor, and they would act most out of character should they strive to attain it by any species of educational charlatanry or any varnish of superficial culture. They are not only willing to hear, but they are most ready to regard whatever suggestions may be made in respect to any improvements in the college system. But some of them are not prepared to initiate or follow any headlong rivalship for numbers which may be proposed, or to sacrifice their matured convictions at the dictation of editorial demagogues, or the direction of the self-styled styled "spirit of the age."

It is their duty to desire, and we believe they do desire to be brought into intimate communication and sympathy with their graduates. They wish that the graduates themselves should feel that the college is *their own;* not as their *property* for capricious experiments and hazardous speculations, but as their *trust* for wise support and administration in behalf of the interests of their country and of mankind. The importance of the colleges, as organized centers of the most valuable species of power, cannot be estimated too extravagantly. The man who feels any obligation to act upon his fellow-men for their good can scarcely find a place in which his influence can be so extensively felt with respect to the most important interests as through a college that has a mature and established growth. Oxford and Cambridge are more powerful in England at this moment than the Lords, the Commons, and the Queen together. As permanent and enduring institutions, they are more lasting than dynasties, and have survived revolutions. If the alumni of the American colleges could but appreciate the dignity and duty of this trust, the country and mankind would have occasion to bless them, and they would have occasion to rejoice in their own wise beneficence.

The wish has been expressed that this real trust, which is, in fact, committed to the alumni, should be assumed by them in form — that they should undertake the actual management of the concerns of the colleges, by electing their trustees in whole or part. Such a measure has been in part introduced at Harvard, and an election is now held at every Commencement, by which a class of the *board of overseers* are chosen by the direct votes of the graduates who are present. The movement in Harvard did not originate, as we understand the matter, in any special desire of the alumni to take a more direct part in its administration, but it was adopted to deliver the college from the interference of a troublesome class of political and sectarian intermeddlers who were constantly introducing into their deliberations, held in public, all manner of uncomfortable insinuations and appeals, intended quite as much for their effect upon political and religious parties as for any application to the internal economy of the university. This board of overseers, though a numerous body, has only a confirming and visitorial power. The corporation of the university, as is well known, is a very small body, and has within its hands the chief, and as some contend the sole, authority. This remains intact upon its old historic foundation. But the movement thus initiated has been imitated by other colleges and propositions have been made,—and in one instance, at least, adopted, to give to the alumni a similar power of electing by classes, at intervals, a part or the whole of a board of trustees. By some, such participation is claimed as a right, by others it is recommended as expedient. We do not propose to discuss this question here, for any arguments concerning the principle or the details of such a measure would be entirely out of place. We have mentioned it as one among many indications that the alumni of many of the colleges are awakening to a more lively interest in their concerns, and we hope to a more serious sense of personal responsibility for their prosperity. We believe that the discussion of this and of every other subject which respects their external or their internal relations will be for their good. We deprecate only that this or any other question should be discussed with the spirit or debased by the arts of demagogues, or that the results of any discussion should tend to drive from these venerable seats of sound learning the studies and the arts which make men solidly great or nobly good. *That college does not deserve to live which would not welcome the counsel and accept the guidance of the choicest of its sons.* We believe, moreover, that there are few American colleges which have any character or age of which the majority of its trustees are not its own graduates. The question is simply whether these boards are not at present so organized as to secure an adequate representation of the feelings and judgment of the alumni. It is a still more serious question, whether the uncertainties of a chance nomination, from a constituency that changes every year, would not on trial give eminent dissatisfaction to the alumni—whether it would not awaken jealousies and strifes which would divide their opinions and weaken their affections instead of uniting their efforts and kindling their enthusiasm.

A self-perpetuating board of trustees, resting on some historic basis, with a traditional spirit, acting in relations of confidence and free communication with the board of instructors, cannot be ignorant of the wishes and feelings of the alumni, and cannot, if they would, refuse to be affected by them. The chance nomination and election of one or more representatives by a body which is organized for an hour, and changes its members very considerably every year, might open the way to constant dissatisfaction and personal discussion, and should not be resorted to except after grave deliberation and inquiry. The alumni of an institution which has prospered under any system of organization and government, may well be content with its constitution and history. If any college has failed to explain its condition fully and frankly to its alumni, from motives of delicacy or for any other reason, let it freely and frequently open to the whole body its position, its policy, its wants, and its fears, with the frankness and freedom which are suitable to a family gathering, and it cannot fail to command the confidence and to receive the sympathy of all the generous and noble-minded of its sons.

Criticisms and complaints are also beginning to be heard in another direction. It is contended that in this country the colleges have unwittingly departed from the original signification of Fellows ; these, in the colleges of England, having been originally resident and charged with the duty of governing, as well of teaching the college. It is urged that, in substituting for such Fellows a body of persons, who may themselves have been uneducated at a college, and many of whom have had little or no experience of its instruction and government, to the exclusion of all the faculty except the

president, we have weakened too greatly the influence
of the instructors. This is not the first time that this
doctrine has been urgently enforced. About the year
1721 an attempt was made to oust the non-resident Fellows of Harvard College and to supply their places by
an election from the professors or tutors. It resulted
in a serious and protracted quarrel. In 1824 a memorial was addressed to the corporation of the same
University, signed by all the professors, among whom
were Henry Ware, Andrews Norton, and Edward Ev-
erett, urging that, according to the original constitution,
and design of the charter, the Board of Fellows should
consist of resident instructors, and giving many reasons
why such an arrangement would be most advantageous
to the university. It failed after having given birth to
a half score of able and spirited pamphlets. We call
attention to these incidents on account of their relation
to the most important of all the conditions of the prosperity of any college. This condition is the maintenance of a full understanding and complete harmony between the boards of trust and the faculty or faculties of
instruction. It is of little consequence what may be
the legal privileges and powers of the three great elements of college administration and legislation, provided they conspire together for its support. A college
in which the trustees, the graduates, and the faculty
are of one mind, and work in harmony and mutual confidence, cannot but prosper, providing there is any occasion for its existing at all.

XIII.

THE RELATION OF COLLEGES TO ONE ANOTHER.

We are brought insensibly by the progress of our discussion to this somewhat delicate topic. The colleges are not in a proper sense, rivals or competitors for the public patronage or favor. They exist for the public benefit, which they aim to promote by the disciplining and elevating influences of that culture, which is commonly recognized as Christian civilization. They adopt substantially the same principles of education and they apply them by similar methods. They ought not to be estranged from one another through petty jealousies, or superciliously to ignore each other's existence or influence. Those which are older and better endowed ought not to assume such airs of superiority, as are least of all appropriate in the commonwealth of letters ; those which are younger and more scantily furnished ought not to be envious or jealous of their neighbors who are more favored by the acquisitions of wealth and experience and the strong associations of young and old. Neither the religious preferences nor the attractions of favorite teachers should be allowed to breed a narrowness which ill befits the generous pursuits of learning and culture. Least of all should a college or any school of learning, play the

demagogue, by adjusting its principles of education or
its methods of teaching to any real or supposed fluctuation of the public taste which it knows to be capricious, and presumes may be temporary. If its faith in
its reforms is sincere and honest it should " know no arts
but manly arts" in urging and defending them. If the
colleges and universities of the country in any way
seem to countenance the methods of political managers
by suppressing the truth, or throwing tubs to the
whale, or manipulating the press, or holding out representations of the truth of which they are not well-
assured ; if they countenance a vicious rhetoric, or appeal to political rancor, to sectarian prejudices, or to
irreligious and atheistic superciliousness, they not only
give just cause of offence to associate institutions but
contribute just so far to the demoralization of the community. The community have a right not only to expect but to demand that those who occupy these high
places of trust shall have a sensitive regard to their
own intellectual integrity and maintain an incorruptible
faith in "the majesty of honest dealing." We are not
averse to adventurous enterprise on the part of our
higher schools of learning. We concede that there
can be no efficient progress without enterprising activity
and bold experiments, but we are averse to the confident
proclamation by any school of knowledge, that the royal
road to an education that is adapted to modern ideas
and to modern life, can only be traversed by entering
its portals.

The relations of comity to one another in matters of
discipline have usually been punctiliously observed.
Most of the colleges have considered it for their inter-

252 THE AMERICAN COLLEGES

est as well as for their honor to sustain the common discipline by refusing admission to any student from another college who does not bring what is equivalent to an honorable dismission. It is to be hoped that the same comity will still prevail, and that those institutions which profess to enforce the spirit of a more efficient discipline while they relax many of the customary forms, will not consider it compatible with their new ideas to open a door of welcome to all those who think themselves aggrieved by unjust sentences under the ancient system. If they initiate such an enterprise, they will most certainly be overwhelmed by a "colluvies gentium" of which the number will be more than compensated for by the infection which they will introduce. It may sometimes happen that a college deals harshly and even unjustly toward an offending student. But such injustice is not often carried to the extreme of refusing permission to another college to make any experiment of reform at its own risk. We hope that the proposed University freedom will not involve a deviation from the wholesome traditions which have been observed between the colleges.

Similar rules of comity have been tacitly observed by most of the colleges towards the more thoroughly organized public schools. These schools are often more difficult to manage than the colleges. Their inmates are younger, some of them are more rude and untamed, not unfrequently more grossly sensual and debased than the worst members of a college ; chiefly because the power of public sentiment is not fixed as in the college by the traditions of the place and the more manly and matured character of the members of the

older classes. Moreover, not a few young men make
the experiment of study and good behavior in the preparatory school and utterly fail. For these reasons
they must be governed by a strong hand and sometimes
with little regard to form. These institutions have of
late been quite as frequently the scenes of organized re-
bellion as the college, and as they become larger, more
numerous, and more systematically organized, it is not
unlikely, will need a more uniform and stronger government. This government should be respected by the
colleges as rigidly as that of sister institutions. In
some respects it is more important for both schools and
colleges that it should be supported than that of the
colleges themselves. Nothing could be more disastrous to these schools than the impression that a senior
class at the moment of leaving their enclosures, may offend against good manners, good morals, or wholesome
discipline and find such offences to be no insurmounta-
ble barrier to admission to the college. It is doubtless
true that a school-boy or a class of school-boys, ought
not to be perpetually excluded from college for any ordinary offences. It may be that the government of the
preparatory school is more liable to caprice and mistake
than the government of colleges. It does not often
happen that such a government is so inexorable as to
interpose its veto in the way of the advancement of the
pupil to the college, provided he makes suitable conces-
sions and apologies. It is not more essential for the
school than it is for the college that whatever position
is taken by the government of the school should be
sustained by all the colleges with ingenuous as well as
inflexible integrity.

Are there too many colleges ? There are not too many
for the whole country with its constantly widening area
and its rapidly extending population. But they are in-
conveniently crowded together and many are therefore
practically useless because they are unavailable for
those who need them. They are worse than useless, so
far as many who need them are concerned. They hinder rather than aid one another by their jealous rivalries ; and their sustentation involves an inevitable waste
of the most precious resources of the country—its endowments consecrated to education and its accumulated
knowledge and intellectual power. The most thoughtless if not criminal stupidity is often manifested in founding new institutions in a city or vicinity that is already
over supplied. It is not difficult to obtain a large
gift from some plethoric donor who is ambitious to connect his name with a new college or university, or by
means of it to dignify the place of his residence or nativ-
ity. In his simplicity he thinks it as easy to found a
university as it is to build a cotton mill, and he finds
no difficulty in securing the coöperation of a zealous
board of trustees and the praises of a gratified if not a
grateful public. To create for the new institution a *rai-
son d'être* some special features are set forth by which it
is to be distinguished. It promises to be especially
religious or especially irreligious. It will exemplify
some new theory or experiment in education, that has
long waited but never found an opportunity for being
put into practice. It will be eminently scientific or
specially practical or more probably both in one. It
will task the energies by severe discipline and high scholarship or provide unusual advantages for manual labor

and varied recreation. There is no end to the "*distinguishing features*" of many new institutions that, *in the judgment of their sanguine friends*, are certain to be speedily *distinguished*. Often there seem to be no limits to the effrontery of agents or the simplicity of confiding patrons, whose money, often given by hundreds of thousands of dollars, had far better be thrown into the sea than contributed to found a "new university" which can only live at the expense of its neighbors. For this constantly recurring evil it is not easy to devise a remedy. Intelligent men should protest against it as an evil and call the attention of persons of influence to its very serious character. It is not in vain to hope that the American public may be educated to greater wisdom by the lessons that are taught by so many instances of disappointed expectations. Perhaps it is too much to expect that any institution which bears the ambitious title of college or university should be content to fill an humbler but much more useful sphere. The need is pressing however of superior secondary schools devoted to classical and higher education. Some of these colleges which are now worse than useless might become eminently serviceable to the common welfare as scientific and technological institutes. Their buildings, endowments and names—whatever these last might be worth—would in many cases be far more worthily employed by being used in the service of a superior classical or scientific school than by being wasted on an inferior or contemptible college. Every purpose which they subserve of honor to their founders or the community in which they exist, would be far more effectually promoted by such a disposition of their endowments. We do not intend by these remarks to depreciate the present or the prospective value of many of the smaller colleges or of the education which they give. A small college well-manned and thoroughly administered has many advantages over one that is larger, in respect of the intimacy of acquaintance and intercourse between the officers and pupils, and also in respect of the rigor with which a few studies, wisely selected, can be thoroughly enforced. The larger colleges have much to fear from the bulk and weight of the mass of material thrown upon their care and from the growing tendency to exalt the professorial to the disadvantage of the tutorial function, to say nothing of the increase of a selfish or luxurious consideration of private acquisition, and of a learned reputation.

The fact ought to be specially noticed that some of the smaller colleges of the country have produced not a few of its most eminent men—men eminent not only in public and professional life, but in science, literature, and philology. It is interesting to observe that more than one institution in which the number of professors was small and of no especial eminence in their respective departments, and which possessed but scanty appliances of books and apparatus, has sent forth in a single year a considerable number of students who were inspired with special zeal for literature, science, or philosophy, and who under its direction and excitements have laid the most solid foundations for subsequent eminence. Of many, not to say of the most of the American colleges it might be said a generation ago, in the words of an animated narrator of the condition of his own Alma Mater forty years before, " Her wealth consisted not in a long list of rents and dividends, but in the ability, attainments, energy, aspirations, and zeal of her instructors and students ; in their mutual goodwill, respect and courtesy ; in the harmony with which they coöperated for the advancement of the institution, and the accomplishment of the great ends for which it had been founded ; in the strong sense of religious obligation that prevailed ; and in the blessing of God resting upon all." It may seem like a truism to assert that these are the most important species of wealth to any college whether great or small, and that without these resources no institution can be a desirable place of study, whatever other attractions it may offer. Many of the younger and smaller colleges have no reason to be either ashamed or discouraged by reason of the greater wealth of those which are older or larger. There is every reason why the sentiment of Daniel Webster towards his own college, which was uttered on a memorable occasion, should be cherished by many graduates of the minor colleges. " It is a small college but there are those who love it !"

The suggestion is made by President M'Cosh after the practice of the Dublin and London Universities, with which he is familiar : Why may not the several colleges of a State or a vicinage be connected together as subordinate members of a common university ; the last being a corporation existing solely for the appointment of examiners and the conferring of degrees ? Each college might be a subordinate to the university ; even its trustees might by their representatives constitute its Board of Managers either wholly or in part. Its examiners might be selected in rotation from the colleges.

If need be the degrees of the college and some of its honors might be conditioned upon a successful examination by the university. No special advantage would follow from this arrangement except the more perfect harmony of the several institutions, their coöperation in the elevation of the standard of good learning, and the stimulus to high attainments which would be felt by the students. But these advantages are most important. We simply present the proposal as appropriate to this part of our discussion without enlarging upon it. We only add the remark, that many considerations of duty and interest might be named which if duly regarded, would bring the American colleges into closer and more familiar relations with one another.

XIV.

THE RELATION OF COLLEGES TO SCHOOLS OF SCIENCE.

These schools are indebted to the colleges for their existence, and it would be unnatural though not impossible that the parents should become jealous of their offspring. Those founded the earliest were constituted as special or professional schools ; the chief if not the sole object of which, should be, to prepare for those departments of life which required a more extended and thorough acquaintance with chemistry and engineering than the colleges could properly impart or provide for. In respect to the requisites for admission, they were placed upon the same footing with the other professional schools. While a course of collegiate study was regarded as a very advantageous preparation for admission, this was insisted on no more stringently than it had been for the schools of law and medicine. Moreover special encouragement was given to those whose previous education had been very limited, to enter upon such a brief course of chemistry as might qualify for some skill in agriculture or the arts, or such a course in engineering and even in land surveying as would prepare for speedy service in the field. Mining was very soon recognized as one of the leading practical interests for which these schools should give a special education.

Inasmuch as a knowledge of the French and German language is almost essential for the successful prosecution of such professional studies, provision was made for instruction in these languages for those who might choose to avail themselves of it. Other branches of study, all looking to some practical application, were added as these schools increased in the number of students and in other resources. The question then arose whether distinct courses of study should not be prescribed, and definite periods for their prosecution should not be assigned. When this step had been taken towards organization, another question arose : Whether in order to prevent this education from becoming too one-sided and illiberal, it was not wise and necessary to make distinct provision for instruction in English literature and history, and in the moral and political sciences. Such provision was made, in one of these schools at least, till its curriculum became " well rounded " into something like organic completeness. The thought had all the while been entertained that such an education was better adapted to a certain class of young men the texture and habits of whose minds and the limitations of whose time seemed to preclude them from the longer and the more valuable courses of the college and the professional school. In response to this call and under the impulses which we have described, new schools were founded and old schools were shaped with the distinct object of furnishing an education in which the English and modern languages should take the place of the classics, and the physical sciences should be the objects of special and thorough research, while a somewhat more practical direction should be given to the studies than is contemplated in the classical college. In this way "the New Education," as it has been called, came into being in a natural way, the demand stimulating the supply and the supply shaping itself according to the demand. It is administered after somewhat different methods in different institutions, e. g., by the elective system of Harvard University, the Scientific School at Yale, the Massachusetts Institute of Technology, and the mixed systems of Union College, Cornell and Michigan Universities.

The Sheffield Scientific School contemplates a definite and orderly scientific and literary training, for the first year in common studies, and for two years following in special departments of study and research. Its friends claim that in connection with the classical department it enables Yale College successfully to accomplish the ends proposed by the elective system without its disadvantages. It has done not a little for higher education. It has attracted a large number of the graduates of the college and put them upon a post-graduate course, giving them the advantages of both the classical and scientific courses and making a reality of thorough university studies. It has certainly done its share, as a constituent of the so-called department of philosophy and the arts to awaken an interest in and to provide instruction for an efficient post-graduate department, or a University proper in connection with Yale College.

A very large number of independent schools have been organized under the special act of Congress, and constitute what are sometimes called the National Schools of Science. The existence and efficient organization of most of these institutions are however to be ascribed to the example and shaping spirit of the scientific school as modeled after the college. Many of these schools are as yet inchoate and unformed in respect to both theory and administration. Not a few are simply training schools for some practical art or employment. A few only aspire to be schools of science proper; connecting with the discipline appropriate to such an object, more or less of general culture. No two of them can be said to be alike either in the comprehensiveness of their aims or the thoroughness of the culture which they impart. It is only the best of them that can come into special relations with the colleges.

The differences between schools of this kind and the colleges have been ably indicated by the author of the two papers in the Atlantic Monthly which have been already referred to. " The fact is, that the whole tone and spirit of a good college ought to be different in kind from that of a good polytechnic or scientific school. In the college, the desire for the broadest culture, for the best formation and information of the mind, the enthusiastic study of subjects for the love of them without any ulterior objects, the love of learning and research for their own sake, should be the dominant ideas. In the polytechnic school should be found a mental training inferior to none in breadth and vigor, a thirst for knowledge, a genuine enthusiasm in scientific research, and a true love of nature; but underneath all these things is a temper or leading motive unlike that of a college. The student in a polytechnic school has a practical end constantly in view; he is training his faculties with the express object of making himself a better manufacturer, engineer, or teacher ; he is studying the processes of nature, in order afterwards to turn them to human uses and his own profit ; if he is eager to penetrate the mysteries of electricity, it is largely because he wants to understand telegraphs ; if he learns French and German, it is chiefly because he would not have the best technical literature of his generation sealed for him ; if he imbues his mind with the profound and exquisite conceptions of the calculus, it is in order the better to comprehend mechanics. This practical end should never be lost sight of by student or teacher in a polytechnic school, and it should very seldom be thought of or alluded to in a college. Just as far as the spirit proper to a polytechnic school pervades a college, just so far that college falls below its true idea. The practical spirit and the literary or scholastic spirit are both good, but they are incompatible. If commingled, they are both spoiled," (pp. 214, 5).

These views we think to be correct, and they indicate the relations which should be maintained towards one another by the colleges and the schools of science and technology. These institutions cannot with any propriety be jealous of one another, for they propose to accomplish different results and for two classes of students. The colleges propose to attain discipline and culture directly, and practical results remotely, though not the less efficiently and certainly when such results are estimated by a proper standard of utility. The schools of science propose to occupy the student with the study of mathematics and the sciences of nature, with more or less attention to immediate and direct

practical applications ; intellectual discipline being secured incidentally so far as all earnest and diligent
study must involve intellectual labor and activity.
They propose also a thorough study of the modern
languages and philology, including the English, for
the reason that these languages are more nearly re-
lated to the uses and needs of pratical life.   Having different spheres, that are distinctly defined, they
need not and they ought not to be antagonistic in
their feelings or their activities.   This being so, the
question would naturally suggest itself : Why not combine the two in one?   Why not unite the college and
the school of science ?   To these questions the author
already cited, replies with equal point and truthfulness.

" But the two kinds of education cannot be carried on
together, in the same schedules, by the same teachers.
The classical course will hurt the scientific, and the scientific the classical.   Neither will be at its best.   The
experience of the world and common sense are against
such experiments as those of Brown, Union, and Michigan.   Nevertheless, they may be good temporary expedients during a transition period, or in crude communities where hasty culture is as natural as fast eating.
They do good service in lack of better things," (p. 215).

These reasons seem to us satisfactory.   The institutions are so diverse that they will act with greater efficiency if they are independent of one another in respect
to government and instruction.   The officers will feel
greater freedom and greater responsibility if they are
chiefly concerned with one set of students.   Their
classes will be far more laborious and enthusiastic if
they are made up of pupils who study in a common

spirit and with similar aims. The genius of each institution will be far more free to form and develope itself if the institution is shut up to its own activities and frequented by men of common aims. The inspiring and regulating influences of the common life of each will be far more efficient if their sway is undisputed. We contend that it is not wise to combine the two, as is done in effect by the elective system adopted in Harvard University. We are aware that President Eliot would explain his apparent deviation from the views of Professor Eliot as quoted above, by insisting that the scientific studies to be elected are pursued as sciences and not in the practical spirit of "the new education," but this distinction is somewhat too subtle and refined to satisfy ordinary minds. Were it admitted, it would limit the attractions of the elective system, and weaken many of the arguments in its favor more than would please the President himself.

These institutions may be separate schools under the same board of trustees and thus exist as members of one university. In such a case they may preserve all the independence which is essential to the vigorous and separate life of each and yet may avail themselves of the assistence and sympathy of one another as well as of the same libraries, museums, and other appliances. Their existence in the same community brings together a larger number of the devotees of science and literature and unites them under the generous relations which are appropriate to their common aims. The diversity of their activities and the distinctive character of the schools with which they are connected may serve at times to correct the one-sidedness and pedantry to

12

which humanists and scientists, theologians and physiologists are alike exposed. An able expert or proficient in any department of knowledge is often more valuable and convenient to his neighbor in a different line of study, than a whole library of books or a series of elaborate experiments can be. Each of these institutions may also avail themselves of the instructions of the neighboring school. Though it is desirable that each should be furnished with a separate staff of teachers, who should be responsible for the most of its instruction and for all its government, there is no reason why the instructors of each should not teach the pupils of the other, in their own or in separate class-rooms according as the number of students and the nature of the instruction may decide.

Each of these institutions has advantages which it cannot share with the others. The student of the school of science studies with the tests of truth immediately within his reach or the end and application of his labors more directly in his view. For either or both these reasons, other things being equal, he will study with greater enthusiasm, more patience, and sometimes with a keener intelligence. Its instructors will have less occasion to arouse those pupils, to whose studies Nature is constantly presenting herself with her fresh and positive aspects to excite to new zeal or to reprove vague surmising, or immediately behind whose examinations or analyses, there lie some of the tempting prizes of active or professional life. He will often be able to make that clear which would be otherwise obscure, by illustrating its working in some actual application, or by explaining its relations to some practical art. Whether the students of the school of science are fresh from the high school, or just graduated from the college, they will be more likely to be earnest, business-like and enthusiastic, than the students of the college. While much of the teaching must be elementary and toilsome by reason of the slow and inflexible minds of those students who are imperfectly disciplined, not a little will be advanced beyond that which is given in the college. If the school of science in some things has the disadvantage of the high school as compared with the college, in other respects it has the advantages of the university over the college, in respect to the character of the instruction and the interest of the pupils. In point of fact, some of the instruction given in these schools has been of the very highest order which the country can show. The absolute necessity of a greater division of labor, tends to secure to the scientific school an important advantage.

On the other hand many of its studies are not and cannot be liberal, in the special sense of those of the college, even if it be conceded that they are properly disciplinary. They are connected by fewer relations with the history of the past, and the ever varying thoughts and feelings of man. They do not cultivate the man so broadly nor for pursuits that appeal so profoundly to the higher manifestations and achievements of life and character. At the same time, it must be conceded that these more elevated aspects of the training and studies of the college, are not within the eye of the pupil. He does not comprehend and often he will not believe in their importance. The college instructor must often labor with pupils who do not always appreciate the value of the studies which are imposed. He labors however with the assured confidence that the results will by and by appear, and that if his pupils do not at present appreciate what he is doing for them, they will do so hereafter. While he contends with special discouragements and disabilities, he has the assurance that the system which he applies has the approval of the wisest men of the past and has stood the test of time. He learns from not a few of his pupils, who have had occasion to prove the value of the classical discipline, that these enforced studies have been of inestimable value, in the subsequent activities of professional, public and business life—that the worst calamity which could have happened to them, would have been a compliance with their impatient youthful desires to be released from these apparently useless studies. He stands fast in the truth expressed in the words of Prof. Goldwin Smith : " Liberal education need not be ascetic or regardless of the usefulness or the interest of the things taught, as it has hitherto been ; but it must be liberal not professional ; its function is to cultivate the mind, and to store it with the knowledge which a youth of a certain class requires as a formal preparation for life. Mental power and general information are its objects and tests, not utility." " Subjects attaining admittance into the liberal course, must prove not only their utility, but their fitness for the purpose of education ; and though the ear of the educator ought to be open to each member of the group of Natural Sciences where it tenders proof of this, the proof ought to be required." He may believe that the study of Nature is as essential to a truly liberal culture as the study of literature and history and yet hold intelligently and firmly that the study of language and of the classical languages is indispensable to furnish the highest and best preparation for the most successful and liberal study of Nature herself —that if a man is to be a philosopher he must in his childhood combine the study of Natural History with the subtle and rigid analyses of classic study. But while the advocate for the classical course contends for its essential and permanent superiority as a means of a truly liberal culture, he rejoices, if his own culture is itself liberal, in the development and prosperity of the school of science. The most zealous advocate of the college system as best adapted to the highest education of the community, is usually the warmest friend of those schools in which the magnificent sciences of Nature are pursued with that zeal, concentration, and patience, which these sciences must always exact from their successful devotees. That man cannot be a truly liberal scholar or thinker who does not rejoice in the splendid achievements of modern science and in the enthusiasm with which its students devote themselves to its service. He cannot be awake to the necessities of the times, and the true enlightenment of the largest number, whose zeal for the Old education, disqualifies him for intelligent and cordial sympathy with the New.

XV.

EDUCATIONAL PROGRESS AND REFORM.

The charge has not unfrequently been urged against the American colleges, by some portions of the American public, that they are bound so rigidly by the traditions of the past, as to be incapable of those improvements which are required by the changing phases of the present generation. No charge is more untrue or unfounded. The older of these colleges were not in the beginning servilely copied from the colleges of the old world, though founded at a time and by men who reverenced the traditions of the venerable schools in which they themselves had been trained. In their original constitution they were adapted to the condition and wants of the communities for which they were provided, and in their growth and development they have undergone successive transformations, according to the shaping spirit of successive generations. We have not designed to protest against reforms in the college system or in its administration. We are quite willing to admit that some are imperatively required. We are not displeased that questions concerning them should be freely discussed by any class of thinkers or writers or before any tribunal. We insist only that the tribunal should be competent to judge of the questions, and that the parties who discuss these subjects should have clear and just conceptions of the ends of higher education, and some experience concerning the means by which these ends can be most successfully attained. The recent agitation of these questions which has occasioned this series of papers, will, we are confident, result only in advantage to the higher education of the country, by calling attention to those reforms which the colleges require, and by vindicating their essential features from the objections of shallow and ill-informed critics.

We are in no sense averse to the development of the college into a university. We believe this to be desirable and possible, with enterprise, patience, money, and time. But we are opposed to the employment of university instruction, and of university freedom and irresponsibility, for classes which require the discipline of the college. To introduce the option of the university, or the lectures of the university, to pupils who are grounded in nothing but in a conceit of their adequacy to grapple with any subject, and who are impelled by aspirations to arrive speedily at the goal without traveling over the intervening space, tends only to destroy the college by substituting the show of a university, and to sink the so-called university into a special school of technology. Were it not advocated in England by men who represent both the aristocracy of birth and of culture, we should pronounce it to be an American expedient, to dignify superficial and limited attainments by high sounding names, and to substitute an apparently short cut over bushes and briars for a path that has been often tried and found to be the shortest practicable. We are not opposed to trying every method and study by the criterion of usefulness, but we would always in-

terpose the question, *useful for what?* We believe that
those studies and that discipline which are the most
useful to train to manly thinking, to nice discrimination,
and simple diction ; as well as to noble purposes, and
an enlarged acquaintance with man and his history, are
the most useful studies in fact : while the criterion of
direct service for the exercise of one's immediate trade,
calling, or profession, is sophistical and misleading.
We do not reject the mathematics from the course,
though their direct utility in the vulgar sense seems to
be more questionable than that of any other class of
studies. At the same time, we question whether, in a
general course, they should be pursued beyond the limit
at which their best disciplinary effect seems frequently
to be exhausted, and their special refinements and intri-
cacies serve to confuse rather than to sharpen the wits,
and to burden rather than to excite the powers. We
would retain the study of the classics, for the reasons
which we have given at length, but we would, if possible, make the study serviceable to the cultivation of the
taste for literature as well as to intellectual discipline.
The design of this study in college should be, not to
train for the tastes and discriminations of grammarians
and philologists, but for the mastery of the ancient languages for pleasurable and easy reading. We would
resist to the last any concession which would tend to
diminish the time or lower the estimate which has
been conceded to classical study. At the same time
we would freely adopt any method of studying or teaching the classics which promises to make them more interesting and more valuable as literature. We hold the
opinion very earnestly that upon the retention and suc-

cessful regulation of classical study more than upon
any single feature of the college economy hangs the
question for this country whether we shall continue as
a people to respect and honor what is noble in the past
or shall give ourselves up to the unsteady and often
mistaken guidance of the unreflecting and uninstructed
present ; whether, in short, our public opinion and our
press as well as our politics shall be controlled by sciolists and demagogues, or by scholars and statesmen.
The sciences of nature have already received liberal
attention in the colleges. The claim that they can take
the place of the humanistic studies as a means of discipline, or that they can even be thoroughly taught and
mastered except in special classes or in special schools,
must, we think, be abandoned.

The claim that the Scientific School proposes a better
education for most men or even a more desirable or
useful education for any man than the colleges, would
seem to be premature to one who reflects how very
short has been the experience of the oldest of these
schools and how very discordant with one another are
the theory and practice of those schools which have been
organized the longest. The New Education, if it had
been in operation long enough for its advocates to define
or describe what it is, has not yet been proved by its
fruits, and it would be the height of presumption and
folly to pronounce it so far a success as to justify the
abandonment of the old system which has at least a definite character and has produced some good results.
Perhaps unsuspected defects may appear in the theory
and administration of the new. The remark of Goldwin Smith is worth considering : " The results of a

training exclusively literary have long been manifest;
the results of a training exclusively scientific are beginning to appear." If we substitute "prominently" for
"exclusively," the observation has no little meaning and
force.   There are those who would decide the question
by contrasting the old education as " the study of words,"
with the new as "the study of things."   Those who use
such expedients usually betray an equal ignorance of
the nature and the influences of the study of both words
and things.   Their position is in principle similar to that
of Rousseau, who would send man back to the barbarous condition in order to restore him to the simplicity of nature.   The study of things must lead to the
science of things, and the science of things must express the thoughts of man about things, and the expression of the thoughts of man about things must be made
in words.   The soul of man in the creed of some people is *a thing* as really as his liver or his brain—the
thoughts and feelings of the soul are as really phenomena as are electricity, or protoplasm, or cell growths.
Government, literature, languages, religion, philosophy,
and induction itself are as really products of nature
and things as cell-growths and chemical combinations.
No man can study words who does not study things,
and no one can study what he calls things without also
very largely studying words.

The modern languages have already been freely introduced into the courses of many colleges.   It is
greatly to be regretted that the elements of French and
German cannot be required for admission in order that
the college training might be more liberal and æsthetic.
For this and many other improvements in the college

course we must look to the preparatory schools.   These are an essential element in the system of higher education of which the college forms a part.   Some of these schools are admirable, needing no other reform except in respect to general culture, as in Natural History, in Geography, History, and the English language.; in all of which special knowledge and refinement, as well as the facile use of some modern language, is more imimportant than is usually believed as a preparation for the highest advantages from the college course.

Indeed, many of the defects charged upon the colleges of the country, are fairly chargeable to the low standard of general culture among the better classes among us, and to the want of thoroughness and breadth in many of the secondary schools.   We shall never forget the remark of one of the most eminent scholars of Germany, the late Frederick W. Thiersch— himself a courtier and a man of the world as well as an accomplished classicist : " The great want of England and America is an organized system of secondary schools.   You cannot have a successful higher instruction, till these are provided."   We believe it to be true, that if the tens of millions of dollars that have been wasted, and worse than wasted, in founding and equipping superfluous colleges and pretended universities in this country, had been bestowed in endowing and equipping a large number of classical schools of the highest order, the colleges themselves and the higher education of the country would long ago have been lifted to a higher position.   Perhaps we should have been ready by this time for the inauguration of the American University—that much talked of institution which so many long to see, and complain that were it not for the stupidity and obstinacy of the colleges, it would have long ago come into being. Will it ever appear? When and by what methods will it begin to exist?

We answer, it will not come into being by prematurely introducing its studies and methods into the college. Nor will it be hastened by overloading the last year of the college course by a great variety of studies, a little knowledge of which is desirable, and a short course of lectures upon which is therefore prescribed. The spirit of *cram*, and of the superficial and mechanical mastery of a few elements of many sciences, is the curse of the colleges as they are. To intensify this tendency as has been done persistently for the past generation is to commit the worst of all blunders. The university will exist only when professors are found capable of teaching more than the elements of the branches which they profess, and when pupils are found who are willing to pursue them with the requisite thoroughness and perseverance. We have a few professors who are already qualified to give as valuable and as profound instruction as any professors in European universities. Some of them, indeed, are so occupied by college work, or by *bread and butter* labors, as to lack the time and opportunity to prepare and give the formal instruction which organized university classes would require. Others have more leisure and would delight in nothing so much as in giving advanced instruction to pupils competent and desirous to receive it. The chief desideratum, however, is a sufficient number of pupils in any one place to furnish an inspiring audience, and to warrant the beginnings of organization. The experiments already made at Harvard and Yale are not without promise. We are glad to see that another step forward has recently been taken at Harvard in the direction of systematic university instruction. The serious *desiderata* in this tentative course would be acknowledged most readily by its originators and friends. It deserves, however, the best wishes for success—a good word for the enterprise which it exhibits, if it did not for its promise of good. We trust that this movement will be followed in the most enterprising spirit in every institution where it is practicable and that special instruction and special classes will be organized as rapidly as possible.

It must be confessed, however, that the number of persons in this country is exceedingly small, who are competent and desirous to receive university instruction in branches which are not professional, and who are also not able and desirous to go to the continent. Or rather, we should say, the attractions of travel, with the opportunity of becoming familiar with two or three European languages, are so decided as to present a very serious obstacle to the development of provisions for any university studies except those which are strictly professional. Not a few professional students even, seek to prosecute or to finish their studies in France or Germany. Of a large class graduating at Yale within a short period, a fifth visited Europe within the first year. Students who have the leisure to give a year or two to general studies in history, literature, philology, or any branch of philosophy, usually have the means of crossing the ocean, and, when they have done this, the expenses of living are lower than at home, and they meet many attractions which, for a long time, will continue to be fascinating to the natives of a new country like ours. It is ridiculous to hear such empty gasconading as has been written within a few months, to the effect that it would not be very long before European students will flock to some great American university as freely as American scholars now go to Europe. We feel no disposition to depreciate American scholarship or American thought. We are forward to acknowledge that some among us have no reason to be ashamed when measured by their peers in Europe. But a great university cannot be built up in a day even in an old country ; and in a new country, not till many generations have provided the material. That material is something more than a few millions of money and a score of brilliant occasional lecturers. A great community of highly cultured scholars and literary men must first exist before the representatives of every branch of knowledge can appear who are competent to teach the choicest youth of the world, and before a large body of American pupils will be satisfied that they can find no advantage in going abroad. These facts should teach us good sense, which is another name for modesty in our expectations and promises. But they furnish no reason why the beginnings of university instruction and study should not be made at once in connection with all the leading colleges. The professional schools already exist, and have flourished for many years, and so far as they have given thorough and scientific instruction, and have required an adequate preparation, have been the *disjecta membra* of a proper university. Let schools of philology and modern literature, including the English, of the higher mathematics and physics, of geography and geology, of metaphysical, moral, political, and social science be added—or, in brief, let a department of philosophy, in its comprehensive import, be added to the schools of law, medicine, and theology, and we have the skeleton of a university complete. We must be content with small beginnings in such a department for the reasons already given.

One thought we have omitted. The sentiment of the cultivated classes of the country must favor the love of learning for its own sake, and the pursuit of study for the satisfaction it brings, and the manhood which it forms, if University professors are to be encouraged by the presence of even a small number of pupils knocking at their doors. As long as study is valued for the money or position it procures, and the theory of disciplinary study and of liberal culture is openly scouted in the forum and the market place, and attacked in the newspaper and the review, so long will the true university be unknown among us. It is in the name and interest of true progress and of real reform that we protest against the supercilious and positive spirit in which the professed guides of the people—some of them graduates of colleges—have treated the aims and objects of education, as well as the contemptuous and ignorant appeals to the prejudices and ignorance of their readers which many have allowed themselves to employ. No argument to our minds is so convincing that we need to retain the old theory and practice of liberal culture, if we would sustain high toned thoroughness in the formation of our principles and high toned courtesy in the expression of them, as the lamentable lack of both these qualities which has been exhibited in many leading articles of the American press, upon the subject of college education and college reform.

We are not sorry however that these discussions have arisen, or that this clamor for reform in the American colleges has been raised, however ignorant and unreasoning it may be. We neither expect nor desire it to cease. We shall not be surprised if the excitement which now moves like a quickening breeze shall rage like a furious storm. It connot fail to be useful, even if its temporary effects are injurious to the colleges and disastrous to the youths whose critical discontent it may stimulate to excess and whose untamed conceit it may flatter into folly. We are quite willing that the whole subject of the higher education of the country should be thoroughly discussed if it can be discussed by those who are competent to judge of its merits. We are anxious that every reform in college education should be introduced which can be shown to be required and that instructors and pupils should be invigorated by the most quickening sense of their responsiblities to the community and the country for whose service it is the duty of both to labor.

The American public, though often imposed on, is not incapable of wise judgments in respect to education. It is the only community in the world which by its voluntary offerings endows colleges and higher institutions on a liberal scale. Its princely benefactors and its humble contributors have had the sagacity to appreciate the advantages which the colleges bring to the public and the generosity to furnish the money which they have required. This public may be for a moment disturbed in its accustomed faith in the desirableness of the liberal education which is furnished by the colleges, but it will not readily withdraw its confidence in the deliberate judgments of those who are competent to decide such questions. It is to such persons alone that our arguments have been addressed. All that we ask of such is that they may be fairly considered.

We began this discussion with no expectation that our contributions to it would exceed the limits of a single paper. But the single paper has expanded into a volume, for the production of which the interest and importance of the subject must be our apology, if any apology is needed.

BOOKS AND PAMPHLETS REFERRED TO.

The Substance of two Reports of the Faculty of Amherst College to the Board of Trustees, with the doings of the Board thereon. Amherst : Carter & Adams. 1827.

Reports on the Instruction in Yale College ; by a Committee of the Corporation and the Faculty. New Haven : H. Howe. 1828.

An Exposition of the System of Instruction and Discipline pursued in the University of Vermont. By JAMES MARSH. Burlington : 1829.

Remarks on the Nature and Probable effects of introducing the Voluntary System in the Studies of Latin and Greek, proposed in certain Resolutions of the President and Fellows of Harvard University, etc. BY JOSIAH QUINCY, President of the University. 1841.

Classical Studies at Cambridge. North American Review. Jan. 1842.

Thoughts on the Present Collegiate System in the United States. BY FRANCIS WAYLAND, D.D. Boston : 1842.

Classical Studies, etc. Edited by SEARS, EDWARDS, and FELTON. (Daniel Wyttenbach. Pp. 246—264.) Boston : 1843.

Report to the Corporation of Brown University on Changes in the System of Collegiate Education. Providence : 1850.

University Education. By HENRY P. TAPPAN, D.D, New York : George P. Putnam. 1850.

Education : Intellectual, Moral, and Physical. BY HERBERT SPENCER. D. Appleton & Co, : 1861.

284   BOOKS AND PAMPHLETS REFERRED TO.

Report of the Committee on Organization, presented to the Trustees of the Cornell University, Oct. 21, 1866. Albany : 1867.

The Cornell University. Second General Announcement. Second Edition, with additions. Albany : 1868.

Letter of President White in the New York Tribune; March 16, 1868.

Classical and Scientific Studies, and the Great Schools of England, etc., etc. BY W. P. ATKINSON. Cambridge : 1865.

Remarks on Classical and Utilitarian Studies, etc., etc. BY JACOB BIGELOW, M.D., etc. Boston : 1867.

Classical Studies, etc., etc. BY FRANCIS BOWEN. Cambridge : 1867.

Inaugural Address delivered to the University of St. Andrews, Feb. 1, 1867. BY JOHN STUART MILL, etc. London : 1867.

Science in Schools. London Quarterly Review. Oct., 1867.

A Lecture delivered at the Royal Institution, Feb. 8, 1867. By Rev. J. W. FARRAR. London : 1867.

Speech of Robert Lowe, M. P., at Edinburgh, Nov. 2, 1867.

Essays on a Liberal Education. Edited by Rev. J. W. FARRAR, etc., etc. Second Edition. London : 1868.

Schools and Universities on the Continent. BY MATTHEW ARNOLD, etc., etc. London : 1868.

Suggestions on Academical Organization, with especial reference to Oxford. BY MARK PATTISON, etc. Edinburgh : 1868.

Inaugural Address of James M'Cosh, D.D., LL.D., as President of the College of New Jersey, Princeton, Oct. 27, 1868. New York : Robert Carter & Brothers. 1868.

The Reorganization of the University of Oxford. BY GOLDWIN SMITH. Oxford and London : James Parker & Co. 1868.

Study and Opinion at Oxford. Macmillan's Magazine. Dec. 1869.

The " New Education." The Atlantic Monthly, Nos. 136, 137, for February and March, 1869.

Culture and Anarchy, etc. BY MATTHEW ARNOLD. London : 1869.

Memorial of the College Life of the Class of 1827, *Dartmouth College, etc.* BY ALPHEUS CROSBY. Hanover, N. H. : 1869–70.

Addresses at the Inauguration of Charles William Eliot as President of Harvard College, Tuesday, October 19, 1869. Cambridge : Sever & Francis. 1869.

Annual Reports of the President and Treasurer of Harvard College, 1868–69. Cambridge : Welch, Bigelow & Co. 1869.

Von Deutschen Hochschulen Allerlei, was da ist and was da sein sollte. Von einem Deutschen Professor. Berlin : George Reimer. 1869.

Date Due

Demco 38-297